YOU
THE CITY

FIONA TEMPLETON

ROOF BOOKS NEW YORK

D1323648

The New York City production of *YOU – The City*, a sponsored project of Artists' New Works, New York Foundation for the Arts, was made possible by grants from the National Endowment for the Arts, the New York State Council on the Arts and the Foundation for Contemporary Performance Arts, by private donation and by invaluable good will, effort and miracles on the part of many individuals. Writing of the script was enabled by grants from New York Foundation for the Arts and Art Matters, and residencies at Cummington Community for the Arts and MacDowell Colony, as well as by much love and respect. I repeat my thanks to all those individuals mentioned on the production programs, especially to Michael Ratomski.

I would also like to acknowledge my many artistic or real-life sources, too numerous to detail, and in a range of forms from literal quotation to profoundly buried influence.— FT

New York photographs by Zoe Beloff
Stills from film by Jeff Preiss
Drawings by Siobhan Liddell
Cover art by Fiona Templeton

Book and cover design by Deborah Thomas

ISBN: 0-937804-38-X
Library of Congress Catalog Card No.: 90-060189

This book was made possible, in part, by grants from the New York State Council on the Arts and other generous donors.

Parts of this work have appeared in *Blatant Artifice* and *Big Allis*.

Performance and reading rights controlled, for permission contact: Downtown Art Co., 280 Broadway, New York, NY 10007.

ROOF BOOKS
are published by
The Segue Foundation
303 East 8th Street
New York, NY 10009

"O einer, o keiner, o niemand, o du:"
Paul Celan

CONTENTS

APPENDIX II—Notes to the Directions (On Structure)

YOU – The City
INTRODUCTION

To the reader:
on the script

This is the script of a play; to read it, however, you may need to understand how its presentation differs from that of a conventionally staged play.

First, the play is site-specific. There is no stage other than the real environments described in each scene; the action takes place on location, and the audience are guided from scene to scene by the appropriate actor.

Second, the play is radically interactive. Only one member of the audience (called "client" to avoid the more misleading and unwieldy term) is present with the actor(s) throughout most of the play; thus the "you" of the text is addressed directly to the client. Most scenes only have one actor, so that the action is mainly one-on-one.

The text, therefore, does not read as dialogue but as a poetic monologue, with the cues dependent upon the client her or himself, or yourself.

***

on reading this book

As a vicarious client you simply read the *script* (right hand pages), the intended. The *directions* given alongside the script (inside left column) are intended to situate the text for you.

The you of the directions is the performer.

The you of the text is mainly you.

The *unintendable* (far left column) lets you eavesdrop on moments from after-performance conversations between clients, performers and production people.

So the unintendable that the intended met as I do you or you me faces the text throughout. Real situations and events, objectively; or with their own intentions; or subjectively, for whoever was you; or whether you wanted to speak as well as hear. Reception is also an intention: what I meant depended on what you thought I meant, and this was what I meant. If I mean, I mean you.

You may read that column and the Afterword, which discusses and derives from discussions of specific meetings of intention and unintendable, in order to imagine the experience of the performance.

You may read the appended Notes on the Directions to extend the imagination of that experience from two dimensions into four. You should consider them as addressed once more to the performer or potential director rather than to the client/reader or critic, as they map practical possibilities, any time, based on the specifics of the New York production, that time. The structure allows the piece to be vertically apprehended and should perhaps be seen as not rules but solutions, and questions I have of you.

***

To the performer/reader: Textual Variations

Variables—marked [] in the script—should be adapted to the specific client addressed, such as his or her sex, clothing, posture and so on. Be observant, not insulting.

Droppables—marked () in the script—are parts of the text that *may* be dropped, if for any client a large amount of improvisation has taken up the time to do the scene as written. Although it is preferable not to drop script, it is better to do so than to so rush the text that it fails to relate to the client. Cut, don't blurt.

Improvisation/Interruption Strategies—given before the directions to each performer. Each scene/performer has a different strategy to use if it becomes necessary to improvise, either to reply to questions or to adapt to an unforeseen circumstance. In most cases, it is preferable to use the next scripted line in such a way that it replies—many of the lines are written as responses to possible responses, silent or otherwise, to the previous line. If improvisation does become necessary, *all improvised lines must use the word "you"*, up until just before the end of Act IV scene i, where the "you" disappears on being handed to the client (see page 112).

***

The Story

YOU – The City is an intimate Manhattanwide play for an audience of one.

You respond as a client to an advertisement for YOU, by calling to make an exclusive appointment. Your rendezvous is at an office at One Times Square, where you are greeted by the first performer, the receptionist, and given a questionnaire to complete; this is the Prologue to YOU. You are then taken inside by a second person, the executive, who delivers the text of the first scene of YOU directly to you, and then leads you out of the building and into Times Square, where you are passed on to the following performer. This third contact constitutes the second scene, which takes you to your next point of assignation. The play continues thus on a journey through both known and obscure parts of the city. Each scene is thus one-on-one, though things get a little more complicated later on.

The fact of which you may be unaware is that when your contact has finished dealing with you, he or she will return to your original meeting point to meet someone else. Other clients will have made appointments at ten minute intervals. Thus you will be but one of a constant flow of clients.

The Prologue and Act I take place in midtown, and besides the above also include encounters with a consumed consumer, a mirror of forgetfulness, a 46th Streetperson, and an excommunicado confessor. The Parodos that follows the first act takes you in a cab, where the driver is the performer, to another part of town. Someone who seems to know you, (a crossover agent), opens the car door for you on a residential street near a small urban playground. In Act II, in the basketball court of this playground, you seem to be exchanged for someone coming in the opposite direction. The next Interact takes you out of the playground to Act III in an apartment, where people arrive and leave mysteriously whose personae multiply, you meet one of you, and you receive a telephone call. (Act III is a play within the larger one, distinctly constituted by its different relationship to the audience, but that's another story, told below.)

A crossover minder who seems to think you want his job takes you back to the wrong side of the playground, where in Act IV, the climax, a revelation and a certain power are yours: it is on being made to wait for the client from the far side that you realize, if you have not already been warned by the fact that the pronoun "you", which had occurred in every sentence from the first moment of the piece, has suddenly disappeared from the text, (or by the client, as you now realize, previously met here, or by someone else who spoke to you on the telephone in Act III) that not only are you not going to be exchanged and sent somehow backwards through the piece, but that you can now be a performer in any way whatsoever to the approaching client, including choosing to admit to the identity of client, which the less advanced one may or may not be willing by now to believe.

The now twin performers offer you an optional Act V, the telephone call back to the apartment, your power becoming a conscious choice. The Exodos admits you to a cafe, where others have gone before you. You can stay there for the Epilogue and the power behind YOU.

Details of mechanics are given under Client Flow and Performer Shuttles in the Notes to the Directions—On Structure.

***

The Story of the Act from the Client's Point(s) of View (Act III)

It, waiting at the house with another, is walked in on by Her, arriving with you. Her is speaking to It but looking at the other, and It is speaking to Her but looking at you. Her and It fight each other into each other's clothes. It who was Her calls Her who was It, Dad. A call comes for the other, and both Her and It speak to you. Her walks out again, on the body of who was formerly It. It, on the body of who was formerly Her, talks to both you and the other, as if you and the other were fighting each other or perhaps death. It begins to take off its coat as if it were its skin. Someone takes the other away. It, with whom, as Her, you had arrived at the house, takes down the clothes that hang at the house, the clothes of Him, changes into Him, and begins to seduce you. Him, waiting at the house with you, is walked in on by Him, arriving with yet another. Him who had been both It and Her is speaking to Him who has only been Him but looking at the other, and Him who has only been Him is speaking to Him who has been them all but looking at you. Him who has been them all knows Him who is only Him, so knows the other, but Him who is only Him does not know Him who has been them all, so does not know you. Maybe Him who is only Him wants Him who has been them all, or maybe wants you. A call comes for you, and I don't know what this other will say. Him with whom you arrived as Her and who has also been It walks out. Him who remains talks to both you and the other, as if you and the other were fighting each other or perhaps love. Him begins to take his coat off, as if going out of his head. Someone else comes and takes you away.

It is clear that you might as easily be the other, arriving with Him whom you knew to walk in on Him whom you do not know and some other. Him you knew is speaking to Him you don't know but talking to the other, and Him you don't know is talking to Him you knew but looking at you. Him you knew knows him you don't know, so knows the other, and Him you don't know knows Him you knew, so knows you. Maybe Him you knew wants Him you don't know, so maybe so do you want Him you don't know, or so, knowing you, he seems to know. Probably Him you don't know is of course Him you knew. A call comes for the other, and Him and Him speak to you. Maybe Him you knew does know who Him you don't know is, and Him you don't know walks out. Him who remains, whom you knew, talks to both you and the other as if you and the other were fighting each other, or perhaps love. Him begins to take his coat off, as if going out of his head. Someone takes the other away. Him with whom you had arrived at the house takes down the clothes that hang at the house, the clothes of It, changes into It, and begins to seduce you. It, waiting at the house with you, is walked in on by Her, arriving with yet another. It is speaking to Her but looking at the other, and Her is speaking to It but looking at you. It and Her fight each other into each other's clothes. It who was Her calls Her who was It, Dad. A call comes for you, and I don't know what that other will say. Her walks out again, on the body of who had been It, who had been Him whom you knew. It, on the body of who had been Her, talks to both you and the other, as if you and the other were fighting each other or perhaps death. It begins to take off its coat as if it were its skin. Someone comes else to take you away.

Her never does scenes ii and iii; her exchange with It is only public, in front of clients, only body to body, with a fight. Him has always turned into It before she can meet Him, and it is she who, leaving the house as soon as she has arrived, though on the body of It, never goes through the Death scene to reach the seduction scene at the center of the Act, where an empty costume would wait. So she never meets nor becomes Him. Neither Him meets It or Her, but only meets Him. But Him finds It as an empty costume; and It only becomes Him as the empty costume, but becomes Her body to body, with a fight. Him never fights body to body but only in refusal, since it would only be to become Him, the same, though he doesn't remember who he is. Her is never an empty costume. It never leaves the house.

It is not until the end of the play that you discover the identities of those you have met; other than the others, all those who come to the house are I, the actors. Unlike Her, It, Him and Him, the 'I's meet and become all of each other. Of course, this was obvious anyway.

Manhattan Cast – May-June 1988

Performer A
    YOU Receptionist

Kachin Kobayashi
Aurora Stiffel-Berman

Performer B
    YOU Executive

Barbara McKechnie
Sharon Goldstein

Performer C
    Consumed Consumer

Janet Giangrasse

Performer D
    Mirror of Forgetfulness

Mary McLeod

Performer E
    46th Streetperson

Greg Arciniega

Performer F
    Excommunicado Confessor

Luis Francia
(Michael Ratomski)
(Michael Buscemi)

Performer G
    Meterless Charioteer

Cecil Hedigan

Performer H
    Crossover Agent

Nevenka Koprivsek
Rosemary Hochschild

Performer I
    "I" Becoming the Other—x3
    —Her,It,Him (& Him)

Ana Martinez
Randy Miles
George Trahanis
(Fiona Templeton)

Performer J
    Crossover Minder

Thomas JF Regan III
Martin Burton
(Steve Buscemi)

Performer K
    Twin Teenagers

Jacqui Mulvey
Glen Venezio

Performer L
    Person of the Crowds

Fiona Templeton

Performers M + (In Cafe, Park, House)
    Remote Monitors
    Fake Clients

production staff
and real ex-clients

Assistant Director
Production Assistant

Michael Ratomski
Linda Peckham

Manhattan Itinerary – May-June 1988

PROLOGUE – *The YOU Office At One Times Square* (MEETING)
Performer A

ACT I – *Midtown* – (IN THE MIDDLE)

Scene i   — *Inside One Times Square*
Performer B

Scene ii   — *From Times Square to the Harlequin*
Performer C

Scene iii — *Harlequin*
Performer D

Scene iv — *From The Harlequin To St. Luke's*
Performer E

Scene v   — *St. Luke's*
Performer F

PARODOS – *Car From Midtown To Hell's Kitchen* (IN TO OUT)
Performer G

FIRST INTERACT – *On To Courts* (OUT)
Performer H1 or H2

ACT II – *At The Courts* (CROSSING)

Scene i   — *Towards Others*
Performer H1 or H2

Scene ii   — *Towards Other*
Alone (cross performer J)

Scene iii — *With Other*
More Advanced Client n-4

SECOND INTERACT – *From Courts To Apartment* (OUT TO IN)
Performer I1 or I2 or I3

(Three variables are given in each of the I scenes here. If a client meets the first of the three performers or sets of performers, he or she will consistently meet the first variable set each time.)

***

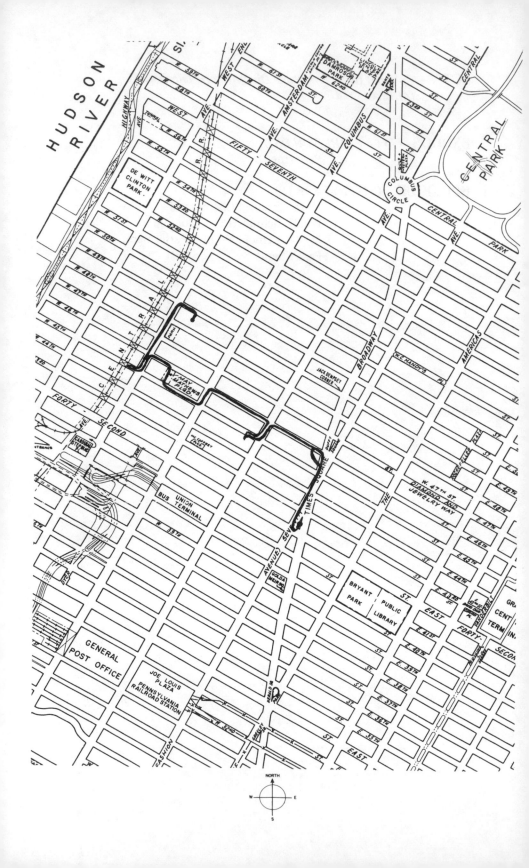

YOU – The City

SCRIPT AND DIRECTIONS

On calling to make an appointment, you are given a time to go to One Times Square. There you are to tell the doorman, "I'm looking for YOU."

PROLOGUE – MEETING
(The YOU Office at One Times Square—Reception)

Performer A

RECEPTIONIST

Male or female. Also monitor performer (see below). Also possible telephone participant in later scene (see Act III,i,iv, and insert on page 136).

A friend of mine sent his suburban ex-girlfriend, and all he said was, "Oh, I'm going to give you something for your birthday, five o'clock, be at this place and go."

It was great that till the end I got to get no program.

Martha Wilson's description of it was that you knew you weren't going to die.

After a couple of years of looking for a midtown office where the piece could begin, we got this appointment at One Times Square where the owner wanted a one-line pitch. We got it. After the show we gave them our couch and leftover paint because they loved the color. We looked even more like an office than the offices.

Action—Unscripted

You greet each client's arrival at the point of rendezvous, though there may also be in-house personnel to assist in guidance to there. You are based at, though not tied to, a desk with a telephone. You verify the client's name, *Your name, please?* and give your own so that he or she will recognize it if you make the call in Act III, and when you are mentioned in the Fourth Interact. You confirm the appointment time of each client, and ask, *Your appointment is at Is this your first time?* If it is, hand the client a clipboard and pencil with the questionnaire, *Would you fill this out for me, please? You can make yourself comfortable.* and have her or him sit down to wait for the appropriate time to begin Act I, scene i, with Performer B, the executive. When the client hands you back the completed questionnaire, put it in a file labeled with that client's name, ready to hand to the executive. Thus you may be dealing with more than one Prologue client at once.

Your demeanor towards your charges and your surroundings should be genial in the unobtrusive manner of one whose concerns are elsewhere, though you focus on the official moment.

In a drawer you keep a small tape recorder with the Prologue music. You can play this as loudly as you wish, but switch it off as soon as the executive enters the room, switching it back on again when she leaves.

Interruption/Improvisation Strategy

Your additional roles as monitor and simultaneous performer should tie up your attention acceptably for most of the time that clients may wish to question you or chat. Besides, your official role as receptionist provides you with a position from which to reply in the accepted modes of client contact associated with the milieu. You do not address the clients in your scene other than as an official receptionist, and then minimally, in the clichés of the job, or open-endedly.

You are, however, open to any questions concerning the client's safety or comfort during the remainder of the play, though it is best not to give away too many details. In any replies to questions, requests or chat, you always use the word "you". Your "you" is official, and impersonal even when charming. This is a job, not your real life.

Simultaneous Scene

You may also have to participate by telephone in Act III, Scene iv, by calling the more advanced client at the house [see Act III, scene iv]. The appropriate client will be passed to you by the performer who answers the telephone there. Script and directions for that scene are given on page 136 [see The Beginning In The Middle That May Have To Wait Till The End] (though otherwise the play follows the order of the client's experience).

You will be advised whether or not to make this call at the appropriate ten-minute interval, by a call from Performers K in the fourth Interact, after they have ascertained whether or not the client in that scene wishes to opt for an Act V and thus make the call instead of you. The call from this performer will simply be a brief signal ("No act."), so as not to interrupt your own timing, if you have to make the call instead of the client at the end. If the client chooses to make the call, there will be no call to you from Performer K. The call to Act III, should you have to make it, will not interfere with your monitoring of the arrivals and departures of clients in your scene, as it will probably not happen often; besides, arriving clients can be made to wait, and clients going on into the following scene will have left before the time for the call, or can be verified and taken by Performer B.

Monitoring

As a monitor performer, you should remain in contact with the remote monitor(s) in the Epilogue at the Cafe, in case of any no-shows or latecomers at your end, or delays you need to effect.

In London we used the boardroom of a major chartered accounting firm. The only people who knew about us were the director and the security guard. They didn't even tell the senior partners because they thought they wouldn't act normal. Our clients waited at reception and filled out their questionnaires along with real accountants' clients. A partner confessed later he saw it on TV and never suspected it was in his office.

In The Hague it's going to start at the European Commission, which is still a kind of mystery organization for Europeans.

(Appointments will be scheduled to include about 10 minutes leeway in your scene.) The remote monitors will deal with any necessary action at the other end of the piece, but see the section on Blanks in the Notes to the Directions for details of passing on the information and possibly delaying entry into Act I.

In scrutinizing the clients, you should gather information to be relayed to the remote monitor performers, if there is time, such as any idiosyncracies of dress or manner, as well as their names. You can write this down. This information may be used later in the play by either performers or clients who would not otherwise know the client, including the repetition of their own questionnaire replies, if interesting.

***

CLIENT QUESTIONNAIRE

A. Your name _____

    Your address _____

B. Why you? _____

    _____

C. Are you now or have you ever been? _____

    _____

D. Isn't that exactly why you're here? _____

    _____

E. What is this making of you? _____

    _____

F. If you can't know if you mustn't ask, why look? _____

    _____

G. Do you know where you're going? _____

H. You see enough of yourself, don't you? _____

I. Do you believe you can act? _____

    Will you yield anyway? _____

    Should I be sorry that I could not satisfy you in person? _____

    _____

J. Are you to end there? _____

K. Does it help? _____

THANK YOU

ACT I – IN THE MIDDLE *(Midtown)*

Scene i – *The Inner You office inside One Times Square*

Performer B

EXECUTIVE

Female? Overdressed for a man, underdressed for a woman, in a sense appropriate to an authority figure.

Interruption/Improvisation Strategy

On the whole, it is appropriate enough in your character to reply in the words of the script even when only remotely relevant to the question. However, since you will be the first testing ground for whether or not a client can ask questions, your response should seem encouraging.

Nevertheless, (see general guidelines to actors) your script is deliberately cryptic to establish the distance of artifice at the beginning of a piece with unfamiliar conventions. If questions are asked about the scene itself, the fate of the client or his or her questionnaire, or the correct behavior, you can use a little corporatese such as:
We will keep you on file.
You will be receiving some literature.
Your input will be taken into consideration.

Action—8 minutes

Having taken the next file and ascertained which of the waiting clients has the next appointment, you greet him or her with a handshake, saying:
(If you know the client, or that line is otherwise inappropriate, use any phrase that will begin the performance with the word "You".)

You are.....?

You take him or her aside to a seat. Your "you" is insistent.

You reach for the telephone but remain poised in hesitation.

You stand and lean towards the client.

"Am I supposed to be talking to you, am I supposed to be answering these questions?" "I don't know what I'm supposed to do."

You rise to leave the office, walking behind the client at one moment and hesitating there.

You wait for the elevator, and go down to the street.

If I could tell you that you are alive . . .

Between the meeting of you and life swings open a page with your finger tracing ordered letters. Nobody gave you the newspaper. Your finger gives you your wrist.

Receiver-fear tests your backdoor "yes". You're visible. Under your sheets, on your mind, your friends let their xeroxed here and nows tell all of you a bigger older secret. Fine thanks, fuck me proper, bread-like and in your unwitting disguise. In the language of which of us? Just as good as being as good as gold as money, count 'em, returning your compliment, two eyes, two ears, two noses alive. So it can't be me you're looking for.

Look. In that meeting where no phones go, why give you what you never refused? Get your desire like you get a joke. Possessed and forgot your punch line? Or don't say no, say . . . I'm rushing you. What you're not getting is in. Don't feel deprived, feel early. You don't recognize your wall-eyed self till you see a stranger. The place is the secret, the sale's in your mail. Not that I want from you, when I ask even I won't. But you know why.

Why you? Why you? The exclusive everything makes you impossible. Bite with your heart the only in two. You can say bad, and bad echo you say, but your ear vanishes as you turn your head to see. I can no more draw a third clenching blank in you. Don't call me your maybe, child of Yes. Yes, you can be your picture. Why is our difference that you're not satisfied that I can't answer all your questions? You know better than I do what you remember, a husband ko'd on the ground, militantly marginalized? You needn't give for me to have your fooling, but your no fooling, oh, then you're a movie.

(You untie the "is it . . . it?" or laugh if you are you, who are freed. You're in the way I wouldn't see, and so I say, thud, you. Something you'll say steps further. Maybe, "If what you now know had happened, your waiting without you would hold time's arm while you burned. Do you count seconds by your heart or by someone else's if you find neither face nor back are glass? Only because your fingers then, like a copy of happiness like your sleeve shadows your hand, never did slide into the nerve.")

Did you see what I saw? Oh, you missed yourself, sister [brother]. But you mustn't know. And I tell you. Because does it matter if I tell you the truth when I'll only speak to you in the smile of the game? You must invent the truth, and you must choose the lie. Don't you see them, like a building and a sky, like you and me looking at you, like a stair with no foot treading, like what you are looking for and what you will look for later, like like, like

You walk to the street exit, not speaking much in the lobby.

You stand outside the entrance.

Changeover

Performer C is waiting, and approaches you and the client.

                          B to client:
shaking his or her hand
                          B to Performer C:
still holding the client's hand, and ending with a glance to the client. You go back inside.

***

I had just delivered a client to Janet, and she was in that super-colored suit. And this guy from the movie theater came over to me and said, "Do you know about that girl, do you know what she's doing?" and I said, "Well, yes, I do, why, what's the problem?" He says, "I'm a detective." He showed me his identification, and he was from a private detective agency, apparently hired by the theater. So I said, "Okay, this is a performance of a play, and she's one of the actresses," and I just stopped right there, because I'm going to have to run like hell to get back up there for the next client, "If you want to come up to our office . . ." He says, "No, no, no, it's all fine."

feeling on the back of the hand, like feeling and knowing, like [fat and blue], like a scary not a person, like security and safety, like freedom from sickness and a machine, like what you don't say to me and information you don't need, like the effort of meaning and meaning it.

It's in the family, running a straight line towards you, different then, a thing you don't know, just one of you pulled towards saying, but not aloud, quite the opposite, but both being true because almost a red-herring, almost possessing, or used to be, intending to deprive, if you will, a part of you and put it in this street, and you dress as the reason, as yourself, as your desire along that line. Your new idea will get older and blurt a moment of passion away from the ear's echo, you or you.

I don't say your name to tell you it but because it's not mine.

Yourself to be swollen with is no lesser defeat.

Recognized you tomorrow is no closer desire.

***

ACT I

Scene ii – *From Times Square to the Harlequin*

Performer C

CONSUMED CONSUMER

Female or Male

Improvisation/Interruption Strategy

. . . . and you are there . . . .and lets you care. . . .understands the world you share. . . .brings you closer to living. . . .takes you beyond the news. . . . and you'll also get, absolutely free, perfect for your bed, your. . . . , your. . . . , ...puts it all right in your hand.
This is an example of a TV commercial you can adapt for your own use. Any well-known public songs, ads, bywords, fictional clichés, idioms, billboards visible as you walk along and so on are suitable, as long as the word "you" features prominently. It is also preferable to drop the actual brand name, punch word or personality, so that while its recognition is implied, the "you" surfaces in its stead. Even embed it in this column.

Your "you" is the most locally (culturally) variable.

Action—6 minutes

You exert a mercenary charm to mitigate your vehemence, but both wear through to the victim as you make your way from the high retail to the lowlife.

You're back. You'll love that sound. Yes, I'd like you to meet . . . you come alone, you're very brave, you've got something. You wanted to come. You wanted to see it. You wanted me to be a nobody. You're talking about you went under cover. You have a whole new identity. They'll change your lifestyle. You'll get a new number. Dead before you get there. They're not your typical everyday person. It wouldn't take you long to figure them out. How do you get somebody to say I'll talk? I think you have to point out that

You constantly invent your "you". You believe (and imitate) every "you" you hear or read.

One guy thought that Janet broke character. He was saying, it's very bad, she said, "I don't want to make you bridle." And I said, "That's a line from the text," and he said, "No, no, she was talking."

This bum came up and tried to panhandle money, and the woman I was with started to wonder, she was just getting ready to go with him . . .

But all these people that were selling on the street, there on Broadway were making screwy gestures, all signaling me away from her, and they came over to make sure I was all right.

14

the tools you have available enable you. Now you see the major changes within, that people are not only speaking about it but writing books. You have the person who's caught in a jam. And that would've been you. You'd be out of a plate-glass window. It could be you. Pretty soon you're filthy rich. If you see an unattended package or bag . . . If you or someone in your family has an accident . . . I'm ready to answer your question. I don't want to make you bridle. You have to compare every other figure. You'll have considerable evidence. You'll sit down with five or six of you. Do you immediately decide? You can't generalize. When you decide, who makes the decision? You can see the way it will literally envelop, you'll see figures popping up. You have surveillance on the outside, you have protection on the inside. You like being the center of attention. You like being the star of the show. You like living on the dark side. You're not really but you like pretending. Billions of you have watched me. If I said you could have this, it's because you don't really understand it. You've got some room. Put in something that really means something to you. Figures you can act on. Ways to make it grow. It takes you through step by step. We'll give you . . . (You want fluff? You were there for about two years. Have you ever come close? You thought you licked it? And they're going to tell you all about it. Have you ever had threatening phone calls? Even if you had no credit problems.) Did you see them stuffing twenties in their pockets and not having enough room for it? If you take a look at the garbage collection industry . . . Let me ask you what happens. Where you stand. I'm not suggesting you can easily. However you have to recognize they're doing it under the guise of representing you. You have to be careful, you know. (Any place you have them longstanding, you have it bad. I want to ask you how you feel about the passing of these guys. You have to have a look at what the prevailing community standards are. Can you imagine keeping three or four million under your bed?) How do you get from where you were to where I am today? Your own guide, everything. Did they say we want you to? I said how well do you pay? We don't know you. You don't know us. We'll know all about you before we do anything with you. Have you ever been or are you now? Do you know anybody within? Have you ever done any business? Is that because you looked like you lied a lot? If I'm going too fast for you, you'll start receiving . . . See you later. When you decide to keep it. What do you do with all your ill-gotten gains? Did you ever get assurance a sentence would be easy? You claim hundreds are scot free. You're talking a lot more than you seem to think. (You never say this but you have to get them out. What was that story you told? About the bird on the plane?) Also you are liable to get one of the nicer things that could happen to you. Do you have one yet? I mean, wouldn't you just die for it? You have to register. I can't give you anything but . . . If you're pregnant, if you're a laid off worker, if you're smoking, oh you're right, you weren't in it. If you get your phone call made, you're thrown in with a group of people who maybe don't like you. You devastate your family. If you realize this, you go in, you're going

The bag lady, sort of.
Well, I had . . . she'd hardly
be a bag lady. She talked
about advertising.
No, she wasn't a bag lady.
The Consumed Consumer.
Actually different people got
different ideas about what
people were supposed to be.
The executives were
psychiatrists to some people.

You have arrived close to a seedy
doorway.

***

Changeover

You smile ingratiatingly at Performer D,
and stand in front of the client.

Performer D slowly moves between you
and the client. Pretending to pretend
not to know the performer, and trying
to sneak off, loudly to the client:

***

in. The world stands still for you. If you don't get it straight. They tell you what to eat, when to go to bed. You do your time. They should let you. I'm ready to introduce you. Brought to you for half. I'll have to tell them you got me here. They might be taping. Of the two people, if you were one and you did it, I'd be guilty. You should pay. You get years. Do all you can. Can you live with it? As our latest recruit you are responsible for maintaining our reputation with the public.

Maybe you don't agree. Maybe you think you're innocent. You should talk to someone.

The most exciting thing is coming to New York and getting in one of your cabs.

***

ACT I

Scene iii – *Harlequin (or Another Showplace)*

Performer D

MIRROR OF FORGETFULNESS

Female. Attractive though not showy.
Direct. Not overtly sexual.

Improvisation/Interruption Strategy

You can use the fact that you can see the
client in improvising, such as at those
points in the text where movements or
physical features are marked [].

Ideally your scene would be exchanged
in position with scene v, so that it would
come after two male performers; but
the attended front desk, as well as the
visibility of the client's own reflection
should discourage literal understanding
of the implied sexual context. However,
you have the most private and
disorienting, and thus perhaps invasive
scene, which the client may counter by
interrupting you. It is important that
you know, therefore, when to become
benign in the face of anxiety or
commanding in the face of subversion,
without breaking your specific reflexive
character. It is probably preferable that
you stick to your text, which is long.

You take the client out of him or herself.
Contrary to some connotations of your
scene, you are, like the other
performers, specifically not an object.

Action—(just under) 10 minutes

You touch the client's arm, "*You!*" and
turn to run up the stairs inside the

ACT I—Scene iii

entrance, past a front desk, and up further dimly lit stairs and into a small room. You close the door behind the client. You show him or her into one of two booths formed by a dividing screen, making it clear that you are entering the adjacent one. The screen is made of a mirrored substance which is lit so that each of you can see his or her own reflection, superimposed on a ghost of the other's image. You can hold your head at the exact place in the screen where the client's head appears, and shadow its movements, or move out of mirror as appropriate.

You speak softly and intensely, speeding up to very fast and slowing to languid or staccato, each paragraph being an arc of crescendo and fall.

Your "you" is disappearing, and so are you.

You call the woman behind the screen the seducer, but to seduce is not an intransitive verb, you need an object; in a way, rather than a reflexive characterization, the people in the first half each had their own transitive verb.

Move slowly into the client's position with the next line. The description is of the client.

One of the best characters was a guard at the door in the studios. When you went up and when you went back down, he didn't blink an eye, he didn't look up, his television was on, it was a Mets game or something. That was typecasting.

ACT I, Scene iii

You . . .

What do you mean?

Of course you were what was intended, but I've had to take your place, because . . . I mean you.

How would you like me to be for you? Would you like me to [wear green, my hair short], surprise you more?

Your name empties, empties, if you don't close my lips. You feel your muscles strain in your [back, your shoulder, your wrist, behind you], curling up your tongue into the fogging words. Where you feel the bucks you squirm them, and with your eye framed open, fire abandons warfare.

What is doubted of you? You're still not properly awake. This close, and you pay no heed to the unseen? A trap would feel safer, might pluck you by [the edge of your clothes], from tumbling through the nothing through which, scattering storebought last wills. Can you find the catch, dear lie?

You could never have answered with your completely other reasons. Every day you're separated further from the door. First your shadow, then what casts you, the power of the head in the fact of the tail. Your half-life is closing

When Glen's friend said to Mary, "I know you," it freaked her out completely, but it's a very easy line to say for a client there. At one point she said, "Okay I'm not going to do it without a bodyguard," so I said, "I'll do it myself." The esthetic and social edges are right with each other in this work; if she needed a bodyguard then she wasn't in control of the edge.

Building to a crescendo.

Laugh, sudden, shrill and long; then abrupt change to low, building speed again.

in on you, you as a place you leave, leave your shadow of a detail. You are in your own hands, you you want less and less to know, no, not really lies, to lie still as you chase your own ball. You block your light. You're not meant to be there, as your so known self.

Were you already so armed in bonds? Your breast rose with my reaction when it all seemed so unreal you wanted to breathe life into me. Throw your mud, yours, because next time, I won't be with you. Die down now, as your water explains to your banks that your presence was required. The eye pitches from the look in yours, slams another, never seeing you, though?

Have you heard how who disappeared? I'm just your thief. (This time you don't need to identify the exhibit, [silk on one side and stripes on the other]. Yours just isn't like that, this, the throat you're close to, milk you're now close to becoming.) How the picture trembles if you draw it. You try to get it out of your mind by [putting something in your mouth], you know, the way you raise your [arm] just so you can show yourself the way. Your secrets are ajar as your stroke seeks another's lapse, but this close you imagine being told, "Imagine."

Maybe someone other than you should hold your breath for you, hoping you could put the two breaths together for ever. (A passing resemblance to you stops, surprised, short of blame, short of recognition, just makes you feel like being wondered at too, bursting up from yourself. You seem to be about to give yourself away, to take on gestures, but your heart isn't in it, you can't explain, you have one bad eye.)

How much do you want to bet with yourself that your shiver of recognition feels the draught of your shame. You draw back your head from a scent you know well. There is no-one I compare you with but yourself. Without you everything I say has no reason, though you pretend it's not for yourself, it's changed into a two-headed face, changed like you.

If your question has a reason, why should this ghost answer beside you, where your eyes look through the barrier feigned like madness of your two new solitudes. If you entered my imbalance, who'd no longer be disturbed? And you'd no longer hear these words, which are your words. As sulphur called to fire, it's not I at the door, but you, once you open. You're my out of control, aren't you?

Your mouth will savor your new silence of nothing to hold you from speaking. You'll just remain signless, to make it seem at first that you have no access, then gradually you'll be haunted, hauled, by the trust that whether or not you come true, this is, sweetness to say, speaking, finally, all of it, your mouth trembling for it. Your tongue trembles up your heart for you to come true.

Take a breath and slow.

You gradually rise, and collect your coat
to leave.

You rise to go.

***

Changeover

You leave the booth, and bring the client
out from the other, then run once more
down into the street, where Performer E
is lurking outside, eyeing the client
intensely. Performer E will interrupt,
still from his distance, and begin to
move forward. Your last words are
spoken very deliberately.

You may pass something furtively to
Performer E to assure the connection.
Then look away, put on your shades and
lean back into the doorway.

***

You keep speaking to try to hold the obscure line open, as if the slightest hesitation would risk my disappearance, and suddenly you'd be there with someone else, to whom you no longer knew what to say, telling them you'd forgotten what you did that day and the story so far, where they figure as yourself.

You hear your own voice telling you to resist. And I fall far away from you, tired of your tiredness. I could hang about your dreams but you want to be completely yourself. If I had interested you, the similarity would have exposed you being dragged along all the more passionately that your future seems so uncertain. The ground is too close beneath you, and a side of you watches your own lips in case of the words I'm afraid of.

You'll think you remember a picture, though you're not seeing one. The [skirt] is your front, your excuse with another's eyes. Who did you steal that look from, behind you as you are now really [starting to leave]. What will be left of you? You search about your [clothing], as if those things that made you who you are had slipped away, though I doubt when I look at you if your hand opens for me.

You must be more than my desire, or this need would see you open the door, walk in, and your hand tighten on my upper arm.

I would sit down in your shadow if this day had a source for this light.

***

If I betray you the next moment, it's because I must, to be faithful to you, for you will have changed. You are in many places, and I am only here, with you.

***

ACT I

Scene iv – *From Harlequin to St. Luke's*

Performer E

46TH STREETPERSON

Male. Derelict.

Interruption/Improvisation Strategy

You have one of the most conversational scripts, so the most usable lines for reply. If the interruption seems to call for a more specific response, reuse the client's phrase in a sentence with "you", which you link to your next scripted line.

Action—6 minutes

You catch the client from behind as he or she steps away from Performer D, and lead him or her down the street.

Be your most charming when the text is fiercest. Turn the cruelest "you"s on yourself. The street is yours.

Your "you" is displaced. You've got the wrong guy. You make the client wish you had the right one, or maybe that he or she was the right one.

Let "you" be yourself here.

You can't.

You have to want the impossible, yes, because otherwise you're not deciding the possible. But not because you want it to be impossible. You can't because you only want, so don't want. If you want to want, you no longer do. You can only swallow me if you're the monster with the bigger mouth. But you can't let me go now I turned within your grasp. You don't want me too close, though, so you dangle me away, your wrapped prey, by whatever you have more of. Do you have time to lose? You use mine. You promise what you might have, till I want you to be able to give it to anyone, even not to me. Because I called you you. Because I thought you called me you when you were calling me him. But then maybe if you'd called me you, I'd never have seen you. How would *you* know? I've said this to you before. So why are you still there? I can't even leave you, see, you're not really you, and yet you're here. If I say the word, you're there. You have to be impossible. Ah, but you have to want the impossible, yes. But you are not all that's impossible. I can want something other than you. Because you are not just *what* I want, you are *how* . . . I want.

You're the monster I never wanted to make. Monster because not entirely separate from myself, I can't walk back and look at you over there. No, the monster is not it, nor separate from you, it's you.

The London version of this character was more of a down and out. Colin rehearsed by making some spare change while he was waiting for clients. He didn't beg, he was just rooting around in old beetroots thrown away from Spitalfields market and somebody felt sorry for him.

In a theater you know you can leave. But here, yes, he's an actor, but so he's a person also trying to break through . . . When it's within a space declared as theater that neutralizes it. Here though, it's primal, it's hard to let go of that other person. I just never considered leaving.

You, like an ugly gift you can't give away, not with the ease with which you can sacrifice yourself, what's yours, and so yourself becomes this monster of viscous parts. Your heart blocks the object from your eye. Who gave you to who? What is this making of you?

Do I seem familiar to you? Am I being too familiar with you? Are you following me?

Sorry to invade you like this. You think I like working in the belly of the thing, keeping you pumping? You're a place that's never in one place, from your heart and back. You want my blood? You've got my blood. How do you keep me here? How do all of you keep all of you here? Because you are the thing, and I keep you alive. But if I died you'd live on. You choke me daily. I let you. But maybe I'm the one who'll abandon you, without a look over my shoulder at you stranded on your own island, with my nothing you'll never miss till you realize your belly's empty, and what runs in your arteries is not your own blood.

Unknown you follow, you're close, you're elsewhere, the voice of other breasting, as in the wind, and the wind in your belly. I can't find you. The air is thick between me and the signs of you, thick between the two gazes of my eyes to either side of you. It's because my speech is only of you that I can't hear your voice. I lost you. You and the wind in your knowing. Knowing is the secret, if you know all or know nothing. You need to be you to breast the sidewalk, the crowd you know. In you, perhaps, is you. It's you who look for you. I find you waiting for me, I surprise you on a stair, in a mirror, smiling over my shoulder.

Do I mean you? I'm here with you. But it's you who make you possible. I have to work on you, till *you* know how you are to be made.

(I have to be polite to you, when what I really want to do is rip you apart. No, of course not, because then you wouldn't be you any more, and anyway, no, I don't want to see your insides. I don't even want to do anything with you, because what use would you be then, for doing anything to me? Till I felt you feel me. I will be good to you. Though polite? No, not your chair.)

(If information is true, can you lose it? Do you have to be good to it, when what you really want to do is rip it apart, because *it* will betray *you*? See *you*? What does it mean when your arm falls asleep and dreams? Don't you believe the polite music of forgetting.) What do you mean by that?

This isn't what I wanted to say to you. I meant in the anger of my reason against you to be right, for you to say. . . . But even as I say all this to you, I'm telling you nothing, I'm showing you nothing because I can see nothing

Greg didn't balance on the edge either, he would go over it all the time, running down the street knocking over garbage cans and scribbling in the doorman's book.

You are the "him". Even indicate yourself.

As I was walking with the fellow Greg, down 46th Street, I was dressed kind of nice, and the other guy's wearing a ratty coat, and his hands were all wild, and what the hell. There were two obvious tourists behind me, and "What is going on here?" definitely was running through their minds. As we got to the church, there was almost a confrontation between me and the actor, because he's saying his last few lines, and I'm looking him in the face. And he takes off like a shot, and almost grabs me or jostles me, and it looks very much like he just took my money or something. I'm looking towards the next guy, looking placid, not acting like I just got mugged, and they were still like, "Should we call the cops . . . ?"

Changeover

You run round and behind the client, at the steps of a church, and laugh facing him or her. After Performer F's first line, you say as you jump and run off:

but you, no you're not myself, and I leave you no-one to say yes to. And yet you see me huge with you. You have to say no to stop me, me who to you am him, stop him. So you can't what? Be you? Let me be you? Let me be you to you? Or see yourself for *him*?

Even if you can never answer me in this language, I am speaking to you because you have become for me, simply, you. Your body can only speak or move by this drawing of me. The shape of your limbs changes, you change color, but I recognize you by my breathing. I knew I had lost you when I lost my breath, but now I can hear yours even when I'm running, and now I'm singing. Do you know who I'm singing to? To the height and depth of you, through the veins and doors of you. And you dragged me right out that door! . . . But who are you to be you? Do you have it in you?

You think I don't know who I'm talking to? Every last picture under my closed eyes is yours. You claim my flesh right out of the arms I think I can give it to. If you can't be if you don't have, whose are *you*?

Later for you.

***

ACT I

Scene v – *St. Luke's*

Performer F

EXCOMMUNICADO CONFESSOR

Male. Very discreet.

Interruption/Improvisation Strategy

Since your speaking tends to the intoned rather than the discursive, your replies could stick to the gestural (closing of eyes, inclination of head, intake of breath, smile). Bent head, folded hands, inaudible murmur, and liturgical humming (preferably appropriately worded or reworded hymn lines, that is, with "you", such as:
O Godhead Hid ... as failing quite in contemplating thee.
... Thy Name Shall be Heard)
may give thinking time. Instil silences. Only as last resort, use Latin (in of course the second person) like:
Dominus vobiscum.
Et cum spiritu tuo.
Choose your spot for a moment of silence.

Action—(just under) 10 minutes

You intervene gently between Performer E and the client on the church steps, raising a tolerant hand to Performer E. Then quietly:

Your voice rarely rises above deep and low, occasionally a whisper, except perhaps for some emphatic intonement.

We were peering through the locked glass door of the church, as I breathed the line, "You don't exist." And crash, there was a perfectly timed rumble of thunder accompanied by lightning and hail.

32

If you can't know if you mustn't ask, why look?

Your power is the mark of my death, and yet you need me as your living fur. You don't exist. You are a pain behind my eye from looking till you're anything I see. I might accept you, but so I would destroy you as I said you were mine. Why should I describe you to yourself? Because you don't believe me? Or because to anyone else you are no matter? You open your mouth to

Even if you can not enter the church, the dispossession is apt and usable. You can see in and you can look from.

The second time I went through the piece, some person off the street joined us and kind of was hanging behind me, very closely. There was a new performer there, Michael, and the man sat next to us on the steps, and was so involved he wanted to get into the car too. But Michael said to him, "There's only room for one." And at that point I really felt like I was hallucinating because ... "Who are these people, where are we going?"

Your "you" is also "You", though You might be "Them" to you. You want to tell them.

***

You may kneel.

When Luis got to that line, "You don't need the big dick," he would often kind of indicate with his eyes this huge building under construction a few blocks up town. So this friend of mine who was working for Ogilvy and Mather realized that this was their new building. He couldn't believe it because he'd been thinking of quitting, and did right after that.

Let silence deepen. Catch the client out of it and into a confessional mood.

Changeover

34

speak and you make room for me. You gulp the world, but already you feel a rough tongue usurping yours as a daughter. I am already occupied by you, but you must take me again and again or else what possesses me is your absence. That I can not accept, because my doing so would not destroy it. Your absence is not offered. Who would you have for dinner if the table wasn't there? If all can enter freely, you're still outside. You pay for the catalogue of your own darkest recognizables, but you stand at your own door in the pleasure of the promise. You're disremembered while you sleep, like a bear that was unworthy, not hungry. I can't see past your not being there. When you're there I'm doing, tossing, spilling. The audience can't stab you, can you? If you'd played more hookey you'd be happier now, when all you want to do is speak straight, your own mouth seen from your own eyes, heard by people eating pictures. You don't need it for your living, words that fall and pile, [a place, a spray, a scale, a window pane] squeaking is a machine being screwed by you. If you're right, you're dead . . . give-away. Your sight stutters your own body. You want to infect it clean, gripped and raised to a smash of applause, to lick that old word in your side that belches sour pictures. You're powerless against the look in your eye, so you speak your empty bank account, till you chomp loony tunes, bad breath, cucarachas, and, unknown to you, you're a place.

And in your place is amazement, love not of the one you give up getting off on, but of the ghost himself. The amazement outweighs the ghost and you mistake a see-through animal for not being there. You shut up and take milk in your mouth with a man between, to blow it out slow. You go down on [his/her] mistake.

No change, no exchange, it's you who are getting better, scarring over, a present hand bridging the two lips of expecting too much and admitting it all. Your pouring shows the contours so you can grip the thought, telling not beating. You're let out. So quit blowing smart and dumb.

You say lean on, you say blow smoke rings, so how did you ask the way in? Fearless invention before a crowd of madmen and scared to say it. Your own forged bills pour in. Forge a presence an absence can quench. You don't need the big dick. A dog-bone being for a human being, just awake enough to know you're not asleep, a valve opens and closes with your words. You're spun to face yourself. Don't say yes.

Unavailable to you. (You swear you haven't had an affair. [S]he should leave [him/her] and live with you. You smile so you know what your face is doing.) Your doors open as recoverings gather. You turn your eyes from what might get in. You're getting the house ready. Your vaulting soars, continuing without interruption into the sanctuary. Is not to taste you your revenge for the bad return on your fixtures? Find room among you for a [wo]man

If you are in the church you open a side door. Performer G is waiting in the car parked at the curb, leaning out towards the client. You look back and forth between the performer and the client.

The client exits ahead of you.

If necessary to make the transition clear, you accompany the client over to the car, let him or her into the back seat, and close the door. If you do not leave the church, to make it clear that this is indeed the next performer, you may nod to him in recognition. The last line may be delivered through the car window.

Performer G will be turned toward the client. You turn away.

of over delicate conscience. If you did as [s]he told, you would talk, be watched, speak, stop getting paid for it, say, say these attachments to your arms as you walk, the skin of your side as though imprinted. I only have eyes for you, shout out out to you, looking at each others' pictures in the dark because you have none, nor a roof. You don't want each other alive, but a scent hurrying after you, unable to understand, still speaking as you climb. Bang! You're pregnant and right out the other side. Again you hear the silences that squeeze the words over, not your fault, you don't even try. You'll see.

You call each other fools as a question with a hellish answer.

Win for you?!

Listening is each other smiling, not knowing it until I see you.

***

PARODOS – IN TO OUT *(Car from Midtown to Hell's Kitch*

METERLESS CHARIOTEER

Cabbie casual, or getaway taciturn. Tape
player with Parodos music.

Male or female. Also monitor performer.

Interruption/Improvisation Strategy

Your script lends itself to reply. Other
than being casual within the general
improvisation instructions, you have no
special strategy. Drivers' conversations
are abstractly personal, and you have
the road to watch.

Action—6 minutes

You lock the doors and drive off. Your
route goes from outside the Harlequin
to near the 45th Street entrance to May
Mathews playground.

As you speak you concentrate mainly on
the way ahead but look at the client
principally through the rear view
mirror. You occasionally turn your head
to address the client directly. You can
also be speaking, or yelling, to the
people or cars on the street.

Your speech seems to be both
self-concerned and gregarious, in that
you ask many questions but they are
rhetorical, or you seem to answer real
or imagined replies or questions on the
part of the client, for which you leave
gaps in your timing, but your answers
seem to be non-sequiturs, or follow only
your own logic. Your text has lots of

I can look back at you. Of course you can see through me. I have to be an impostor, though you don't know of what. But you do. And where do you fit in?

You're in your place. You're not a thirsty [wo]man with a picture of water. You can quarrel. You can lie. Can you tell a lie without a story? You think I'm repeating myself instead of telling you a story.

Can you travel only towards and not unite, untie? You're not looking for the heart, then, nor the other side? How do you know if you'll see me again? But do you have to go home to leave by the back door?

Why answer now when you're paying? Do you want forgiven in advance? You don't have to be taken out of yourself, you're out in yourself. You're too cut up to argue. You'll edit in your head. It's your prerogative. No, it's your head.

*Did the car ever get stuck in
traffic?*
*Usually Cecil had more than
enough time to get there, so
sometimes he'd take people
way up, he'd be up in the
50's already, asking the way
to the bridge, before he'd
turn round and get back on
his way.*

*"I won't walk around here.
Where are we going?" And
what could you do with
them? One woman refused
to get in the car, because
the back was full of beer
bottles, and she'd always
been told not to get in a car
with a stranger, but then it
was better than being
stranded.*

breathing-room for the client,
driving-room for you.

Your "you" is often "one", so sometimes
"I", meaning you.

Do you think my story's the same as the next guy's? Do you care? This isn't pointing at you, you're in it, (like your mineral clothing, your crawling breath, your prosthetic employment, your history I don't want to know. Are you one of those who write your name on dollar bills? Do you caress the electric? Does it recognize your touch? Accuse yourself for this language with waste meaning. It's bigger than you.) You're a limb of the monster dismembered because you're not looking back.

Watch where you're going. I don't want to be stuck with you forever. Aren't you hungry to move on? If I look away are you free? Now you can see more than two sides of life, like leaning into the mirror after your night on the tiles. What's in it when you're not? Out there is your way in.

Are you awake? Here you never sleep. You're halfway, though you're turning from the straight and narrow to the here and now. (Do you need me then to find your way when it comes to you? How does your speechless weakness choose a difference as a place? Do you know who I am? You don't leave home with me. You have to get in to get out. I'm only time to change your mind. You can't sneak in when there's no wall. You can't be murdered if you've never been born. Being alive in the future means you'll stink more.)

Is your answering machine on? You're close to transport. You describe maps on the telephone. Your state-of-the art screen fatigue is a science of the state fatigue screen. You save, slow, stop. You read the image of a finger because you know there is a way. You escape, merge, yield. You are mutual shadows reading where only your error echoes obscene orders. You hit delete and go to jail.

What's a secret when all you need to know is the command? What if you did what only one person told you to do and you didn't have to? Did you ask anyone else what their problem was?

You can see what you don't have. Do you know where you're going? Do you make someone else's love? Would you recognize all the parts of your body? Like the back of your hand, the street's knowledge. Give them my regards when you see them. Your piecemeal measurements burn back at you.

Are you framed or before your time? Hiding your eyes from this or this from your eyes? You know this is dreaming because you saw it on TV. There's nothing you're not supposed to see. Be glad if it's possible for you to betray, be glad if you can be caught. But don't you try. Is the least resistance yours? Your feet are up.

Have you noticed how [the one behind there moves what he touches (something happening on the street)]? If you're not at the top you're

There were quite a few improvisations that weren't in the text, in fact people were referring to the color of the shirt I was wearing, and my sunglasses.
Well, in the text there would be written, say the color of the guy's shirt or something like that. It depends what you mean by text.

London cabbies have to learn the streets of London for years before they can take the test. "It's called getting the knowledge." People would always ask Marcus the way and he wouldn't have a clue.

You have already pulled up and have been addressing the client in the mirror. You turn and lean towards him or her.

***

Changeover

You have arrived near the entrance to the park, where Performer H will be waiting. Flash your lights to let her know that you have completed the text or your timing, and undo the door locks. She will approach the car and open the door for the client to get out. You drive off.

***

underground, like any building being eaten out. You're off-scale squatters in a path-jungle. Do you make a left or a right for the river? You don't need to understand to be answered. To persuade you I use the word "already". I'm not who you think, you think, but how can you tell a building from the one in its windows? You'd find the same from the inside. Sophisticated people don't ask questions, do you? Caught you! No, I wasn't disagreeing with you, I was talking about something else. Yet you take the words like quicksilver right out of my mouth. Who will I tell about you?

Don't you drift off. You mustn't lose me. Do you think it's *my* spirits I'm trying to raise? How would you know if you'd been mugged or had a brain storm? You've got to get out to get in. For all you know it stops there. People look at you. You're visible on the edge of the round world. Too real, you're asked, not out, but if you've been out. You ask to be held. You're making nothing, you're moving or watching moving or watching watching or seeming watching. Does your new redundancy put meaning out of business? Did you finish...?. I can't face you... if you're going the same way. But I don't need to watch you if you don't take your eyes off me. It's two-way traffic once you get to the bridge. You're in the shit. You've been arranged. I'm saying this to turn you around.

Why shouldn't you be asked who you are, though you know? What becomes you? What do you become?

***

FIRST INTERACT – OUT *(On to Courts)*

Performer H

CROSSOVER AGENT

Initially camouflaged to surrounding people. Close.

Female. Duplicate performer. Two scenes.

Improvisation/Interruption Strategy

Your conspiratorial mood allows you to listen and take into consideration without replying particularly literally, so your text can be used for most replies, perhaps with a glance around or a posture of particular effacement as if you are breaking rules.

The one point where you may have to be literal is at the crossover.

Action—8 minutes for interact (5,3), with total 11 minutes this performer

You open the car door for the client, smiling, and immediately intimately conspiratorial. Maybe you take the client's arm. Every now and then you look around, acting as if acting as if nothing.

Your manner is charming to allay suspicion, gradually becoming suspicious and knowing. Your "you" too. You both know already what you're talking about, so you don't need to talk about what it is.

You seemed to be having quite a talk with yourself. I'm only here for you. You're an end in yourself.

I do wonder every time if you'll come, like a wound salted by each seatide.

I'm not supposed to talk to you about this. I couldn't exist if you couldn't walk right through me, and you couldn't get through if you didn't really see me. You see enough of yourself, don't you? There's more than one way you can say no to me. I can't spare you. You're in the same place as me. There has to be someone to whom you can tell everything, even if you don't, even if you don't know how, just for your own sake, doesn't there? I'll be waiting for you. You'll be waiting for me. I wish you could tell me but I know you can't. Maybe when you're free—if you're ever free.

If you have to call a tow truck for the big motor, because you think about liking while driving . . . you're all over the road . . . You try to explain. You know how it is in this sort of business. You're afraid to say anything in case

Move behind the client.

you're either wrong or wrong to say it. Sometimes the hardest is to act the way you feel. How many times can you bang your head on the wall?

If you're anxious to go somewhere, does that mean you're being watched but you've been told not to bolt, like a flash of lightning in the night, you disappear into what you said, you, what's your name, you. No one else can hide like you. You have to bear with me. Wouldn't you want to know if you were seeing through someone else's eyes? How many are missing when you're not there?

I wonder what you were told. Why should you only ask questions about the past in things? If I just tell you some story, that won't be you really knowing because you're always being told stories. And yet it's all some kind of a story for you, (you see the true crossing the untrue, making the possible, many possibles, according to the number of lies, the amount of maybe, the you in the first place.) But if there's you and me, we have to agree on a few things. Though you wonder if you can ever be the same twice. You're the reason I trust myself. (Is it a woman you're after? Is it questions you want asked?) You're not halfway. Or half your time isn't up. I'll get through with you. I'm not pulling your leg. I'm just remembering things you don't. Weeks and weeks and weeks of your breakfast in your mouth. You're not eating it. You're talking it. And so is the person across from you.

Did you ever steam open a letter? Of course, once you knew the answers they'd no longer be yours. The gradually knowing what you're unable to know, that's what's really yours. Unless they want you to know. And yet you're not really your own if you're not able to keep watch over what's known of you. I wonder what you really think of, how much you can know. (Can you say, and I'm not asking you, you can memorize lies more easily? If you make people up, do they mean more? I mean you. It wouldn't be a secret if I told you. You wouldn't know it was a secret if I didn't tell you. What's given to you is thrown everywhere, and you turn, and turn without moving until you receive, precisely.) You lie open. Do you lie? You say nothing. I'll tell you no lies, though it won't be easy to tell you the truth.

As you can see I've been following you closely, though I never thought you were looking back so much; though I never thought you'd keep so much to yourself. I thought you were having fun. Does that hurt you?

Do you never find that you shock yourself, that you've done it again, or said it? What, you ask? No one could say you were wrong. If I mean it, do you have to make sense? You get each word away from the others and everything you thought falls through the spaces.

I know you're not me. Who am I, you want to know? I'm who's talking to

Even though it's not the fantasy that you could have wanted ahead of time, things are happening in your head and before your eyes that feed into a wish fulfilment...

There were clients for whom it wasn't manifestations of desire at all, it was absolutely manifestations of their worst fears. They weren't afraid of what would happen, but of not knowing what would happen.

Ad absurdum.

***

No Changeover

You have reached the southern part of the basketball court (see crossover diagram). You and your client hesitate for a moment at this point, looking up and ahead to where you see two people hesitating symmetrically at the northern end (Performer I and a more advanced client.) You deliver the following short part of the monologue standing face to face with the client. The scene after the static speech is otherwise a sort of continuation of the previous one.

***

you. Oh, of course I always change, I change toward you. Because there are different ways of finding you. You think you could find your way? Do I change for you? You tell me. Do you think I would say the same to you as to any other? If I speak to you I'm telling you who I am. Or am I asking you who you are? Maybe I seem to be telling you who you are. I won't say I know who you are. Maybe I'm asking you who I am, but how would you know? From who you are, or seem to be to me . . .

You're not discussed.

* * *

You I'd call on, because with you there is no game. If I need you, you can need me. With you there is no debt. For you my hands are empty. To you my heart is emptied, as your body fills it with ourselves. Your smile fills it with elsewhere. For you my body is bathed, and your eyes clothe it with my smile. My excitement confirms yours. I need not possess you, because you will never withdraw. You may turn to another, but never away from me. And the mystery of my other you makes me mine, you meaning I don't understand, not you meaning I do. I need not be you. You don't seem myself. You must be you. So I will be like all of you, because you open and do not divide.

* * *

ACT II – CROSSING *(At the Tracks)*

Scene i – *Towards Others*

Performer H

As previous scene

Action—3 further minutes, partly including crossover

You and your client continue to walk towards the approaching two people. You both know who both of you are, though perhaps not each.

Meaning you, at first.

You move close to deliver a cryptic message,

and draw back at the client's reaction (whatever it may be), with a change of mind:

Oh, by the way, you know how we like to keep these things between you and me. And I couldn't do this without you.

Going over to the other side means you didn't want to want. You go, you stop, you go, you stop, you go. You don't stop. And you won't. You can't exchange everything. It's not my way you'll find. I never told you much. You thought I did. And maybe you were right in a way. Perhaps that was all there was to tell . . . you.

You're dumb if you can't be heard. But you can tell the truth in a way. Something can happen from you. Do you think you're dangerous? You're all dangerous, and you have to accept your power. Even the power to make no difference makes you part of the most powerful. Because you make the same bigger. You're committing nothing. That makes you a big sinner.

(Will I help you lose your nerve and give in to it all? There's nothing unusual in being afraid they'll tear you to pieces. Do you think they really exist? Why don't you talk to them? See what you can pick up. I leave it up to you.) I promise I don't want you troubled. All the same, you're here now, so you're the obvious choice. You'll be a surprise, and you'll know what not to give away. No one else has your open facade. You pick up your look from whoever's talking to you. You're my right hand in this. You've got it wrong. Is it just as well for you to believe it? Do you accept that? Do you need it? Is this your spare time? Are you asking me?

So, you've been confided in.

I got into this thing with the actress as if we were both pretending that nothing was going on, and I wasn't sure if I was pretending nothing was going on in reality, which made it really feel something was going on, or if I believed her acting and was acting too.

The second half in London was in a mainly Bengali area. There was a street demonstration around there on our last day. It was protesting some killings, allegedly racial, and the teenagers turned it into a bit of a riot later on. We tried to keep a low profile, though we had kind of been locally accepted by then, but some clients thought we were just being fictitiously cloak-and-dagger. Until they saw the beat-up cop.

Changeover

You and your client have reached a point where the way is clear across the side of the basketball courts. You both stop, as do the two approaching people. You remain where you are while your client is to continue on towards the other two. The client should have got this idea from the preceding monologue, or you can further clarify it if necessary at this point through improvisation; you can give him or her a gentle shove and turn your body away, with a look to where one of the other two is coming in your direction.

***

Nor are we in this together, you and I. My bond is to you, and yours is . . . to you. Even if I hold you there, to suffer your own pleasure.) That too is you, knowing how I've known you, not just when you no longer want but when you no longer are.

You almost begin to scare me. If you knew what I meant, I wouldn't have to tell you. You wouldn't exist. It's not for me that I'm exchanging you. Your people ask it of you. My New York isn't yours. My words can be translated into yours, but they're not yours. You fear and yet long to cross that line. You're expected. Your route is carefully planned. It's coming towards you. I won't keep you.

***

ACT II

Scene ii – *Towards Other*

I had decided I wouldn't betray anything, like walking down the street. But it all fell away. Somebody would say something to me and I'd respond. It was like various sides of my own brain talking to me, because several times people said what I was thinking. It was like these children's books where parts of it pop out, I was in the middle of the city and all of a sudden that two-dimensional world which I know is three-dimensional but is always two-dimensional as I walk around, suddenly became three-dimensional. I remember standing in that kid's playground, and thinking, what a set. Like if you look at a painting by Rauschenberg or Johns and you have painted parts and then you have a real broom stuck in, and you think, what is that doing there?

(Performer I)

In a sense, there is no performer in this scene, as the client walks the distance alone.

However, Performer I is a hidden participant at the far end, in order to monitor the actions of the unaccompanied clients.

Action/Changeover

The scene consists of the changeover between scenes i and iii. The client leaves Performer H and walks towards the people who have been approaching. Meanwhile, one of those two (in fact Performer J, although the client will not be aware of this fact) leaves the other and walks towards Performer H and her client.

Performer J and the client cross at the very center of the side of the courts, without communicating.

The client continues along the tracks to join the more advanced client at the northern side of the courts. (The success of this changeover scene rests on the assumption that, judging from previous base scenes the client will take the person he or she is approaching to be the performer of the next scene.)

***

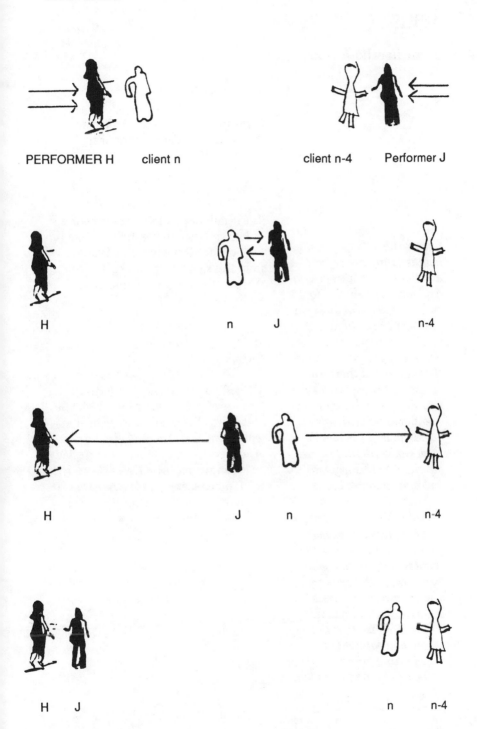

PERFORMER H   client n   client n-4   Performer J

H   n   J   n-4

H   J   n   n-4

H   J   n   n-4

ACT II

Scene iii – *With Other*

(Performer I)

Performer I is a hidden participant in this scene in order to monitor the actions of the two clients.

Action

Clients started hallucinating performers, and thinking, is this person a performer? I started to pick out the client look. One time I tore over to the park—I wore out my Reeboks, I got new ones for the show—and there was no-one but Glen here before me, and I said, where's the client, and he said, there is no client, and I got really mad, Goddammit, I rushed. I went up to this woman, and said, "Excuse me, are you with YOU?" and she thought that was hysterical. I said no, this is a serious question. It turned out the client was right there and heard me go through my whole aarghh, so I went over and smiled and said, "Hi, you realize that the person you thought you were looking for has arrived . . . ", and pulled him away.

The details of this scene are of course unknown, since the participants are both clients. If the two clients stray from this route, they will be guided there at the end of the scene by Performer I.

Changeover

The less advanced client is taken by Performer I, who will know which one of the two clients this is as he or she will have already been met in the apartment. Any error can be corrected by Performers K, who have also watched the last two scenes, and who now take the more advanced client.

***

SECOND INTERACT – OUT TO IN
(From Playground to Apartment)

Performer I

"I"

THE OPPOSITE

Male or female. Triplicate performer. Five scenes.

Improvisation/Interruption Strategy

Your strategy will be very different in the Interact to the way you will be able to deal with interruption in the Act, since you will have the rhythm of the other performer to consider there.

In the Interact you relate through both a slightly alienated text and direct address, so your only diversions from script need be to include some real life.

Action

(You may have had to intervene in the changeover from the preceding scene, if the two clients strayed from the expected route. If so, you would remain with them both on an improvisational basis until you are sure that Performers K are ready to take the more advanced of the two when you leave with the less advanced client for the next scene.)

You take the client out of the playground and towards the house. You start this scene funny and unhelpfully explanatory, to get serious later on. Include a lot of seeing the environment as support of your explanations.

I don't think it would have worked if one person had performed the whole thing. You would have overloaded very early and be you-ed out. Those performers who were with the client longer had more than one strategy. I was Performer I, but the role lasted as long as the idea of a particular line or a particular sequence.

You realize that the person you thought you were looking for has arrived at the place you just left.

You're unfolding what you didn't have till now, time like a map because now you can pay with it when you've been shown you'll be seeing the same thing differently. You can't have been there if you're here. You can thank somebody you haven't met yet. What there is to know is that you know what I don't. You're told who tells.

I had fans on every corner, every old Puerto Rican guy on the block. Yeah, "Hey, Cat Lady" was the favorite, and I'd be ignoring them.

At "even if you don't know whose limo nobody saw you leave spit on", nine out of ten times there was this huge limo that would pull right up. Or "the wrong face . . . though someone else wears yours" and we'd look in the park and all these people would be there staring at this client.

You will be in one of two personalities, Him or Her (see Act III). Neither of these is really you, nor fully played during the Interact. Who *are* you? For the moment, you are some person, reintegrating the client after he or she has been with an extratextual being in the playground. Your text is shortish for the scene, so once the script is re-established, you also have time for silence.

(The Skyline is a hotel sign against the skyline.)

The color of your face comes back. Look. Do you think I invented this body? What if you were asked, take me to your leader, singing, Love that within my mind doth discourse hold, or drawing a landscape by a cake recipe? If you knew the end, there wouldn't have been a double-breasted wanted sucker to do time.

Look. Your shadow divides the light into a list of what you can see. You're wanted. On the inside, you get off on putting bodies together, so do you think I'm alive? What's whispered to you here is really said. You can choose to hear me talking or hear what I'm saying. I tell you I've got you covered. Do you think it's fair? Are you playing a game or do you only want to know who else you could have been? You want someone else to want who only wants, a kid cracking IBM into your bank account for fun, not out of your veins. Do you want to be asked who you are? Show me any part of your body your heart desires. And you doubt, and teach darkness you won't catch the germ, your palm filled and dwindling, my bed's uprising grabs you up. You coincide like panic with a fruit-core at the door. You're marked. The sidewalks seem like ledges to you, but you know they're not an organization.

Look. Can you read the Skyline? One more swelling on you or a way you divide your head from your legs? To preserve your clean mouth from flaunting art? Can I compensate for blood? Can you go for the gold without it, a place without the shading of choice, people pretending they have to be this close to you, even if you don't know whose limo nobody saw you leave spit on. Your resume engenders the dash you cut, the raise you doubt, the antechamber you pardon, the shift you untie, the shit you boil, the little simple soul you dress up down in the dumps of your will when every morning marks your body, in and out of knowing you. Do you need introductions or might you deep-cleanse the wrong face, even if you can't hate it though someone else wears yours. You punch in the corrections of your care sideways and out, and the corner you turn faces the crowd coming up from underground. They look to you as if they're trying to leave something. Do you run or do you think till you sink, your arms trying to stutter a fiction? If they always did you'd know you were always going nowhere, and nowhere was where you went. You pretend to resist to stay close. Your poor or stingy body figures the countersign.

(Am I kidding you? Would I risk your not forgiving the scentless night prowl your fear breaks, wasting through locks on what you did to what was valuable? You translate hard-core grace as crude climbed beggars. You're in the light, not yet decided speed and speech's horny gobbled names.) You try to memorize so you can decide later you can forget, so no fruit rounds your fingers. (Mama, what do you want? You watch yourself get skinny and steam comes out your mouth. Would you wash your hands before or after touching? Do you hear in capital letters? Whoosh. I keep telling you the

*There was one little girl by
the other playground on
47th St, she couldn't have
been more than about 15 or
16. And she said, "Baby, let
me see that glove." I gave
them to her, and I said, "Be
careful, they've got holes in
them," and the little girl
looks at me, and I says
"Well, you know, I wear
these as my alter ego," and
she goes, "What's an alter
ego?" And I says, "Well,
when I wear them I turn
into another person, it's
part of my act." And she
looks at me. And the black
girl starts telling me that I
should take the fingers off,
and I say, "No, no I need
them for the rest of the
play," and she goes, "You're
in a play?" I say, Yes, and
she says, "We thought you
were working!"*

Changeover

You arrive at the house and knock on
the door, or window. You do not change
over to a new client at the end of this
scene, but remain with this client while
you also join the next client ahead as
well as Performer I ahead.

***

time is set hard. Is that how you conform to dying? Or by changing into something else, words with words, you think. You think, how do you know what people sounded like to people then?) People will figure the hairs you're pulled by. You're hung up, you lie down. You're not ruled, you're managed.

Look. I won't tell you I can see the moon because we both know it's too early. You're your boss. (If I wanted you to want to understand how I'm under your skin, how another language is a fun you have to have, how this ground is what your thirsty foot wears because not enough different people scares you, you'd know why I'm anxious for you to write to me.) You're great. You leave. You move so you're sold. If you can be wanted you're in style. O come, o come, not you, what of you, as long as you can tell you're you, you sweet slum software? Dare you? You don't sleep. You have no things to change. Your stripped class strips back your apology to words over you.

You hold me to it. That's your jail. I can't pretend you can't describe me, describe me away. Will you be told close looking is sleeping? Do you believe you can act? Are you on a local channel? How much do you charge? Even so, you give what you get. You don't get your behavior free. You can cross my palm but not with the redundancy of your memory. If another time is another place, I ask you, can you leave? Are you early?

***

ACT III – INSIDE *(At the House)*

The Play within the Act

It is important that while the instructions in this act are addressed to Performer I (1, 2 or 3), the scenes are given in the script in the order in which they occur for a client, not for the performer. Every other client also experiences a different order (See the story of the act from the client's point of view in the introduction to the script).

Performers I1, I2 and I3

There are four costumes: HER, IT, HIM AND HIM. Him and Him are identical.

All three I's are actors, dressed underneath their costumes in simple black.

It is a bear costume. The other costumes are gender-specific. Him can be worn over Her.

Scene

The room contains a telephone in a corner near the door (or in another room there). A table is close to the door. Between the table and the door there are two chairs, facing each other, and, slightly obliquely, facing the door and mirror. Along the walls are couches or chairs, and mirrors above them on at least two walls. The lighting is directional.

Most of this setup can be arranged in any real room. Decor is as found, or none.

Scene i – *With Three*

Performer I1 (as It, waiting) and
Performer I2 (as Her, arriving)

The bear head makes eye contact
difficult, so this can be compensated for
either in gesture or by the other
performer.

The style of action is not affected by the
costume, unless mentioned. The bear is
particularly human in movement, and
often frozen, the other performer doing
most of the action.

Interruption/Improvisation Strategy

You are an actor, and have almost
become the first object-performer, so
stick to the text, except for emergencies,
in which case deal with the client (in
scenes i and iv, preferably the other
performer's client) as if he or she is
yourself. You will probably have to
improvise physically, in manoeuvring
clients. Scene iii might elicit more
response, to which you have many
physical resources to reply with.

Action—4 minutes (totaling 10 minutes
for scenes i,ii,iii or iv,v,iii)

Except where otherwise noted, you
address the text to the client who
arrived with the other performer, i.e.
Performer I1 to the less advanced client
and Performer I2 to the more advanced
client, who begins seated facing the
other seat, and so facing the mirror.

The clients are on the *outside* of the
centrifugal action.

Lines included within brackets { are
spoken simultaneously.

ACT III, Scene i

standing near the mirror:

approaches less advanced client in a circle around the chairs, moving him or her into the room:

moves away from less advanced client, back to mirror:

In the house, when there were two clients and two performers, a lot of people would relax, because a lot of people had their friends come after them, and you could see they would literally go, Oh thank god you're here . . .

turns, extends paw to mirror:

I arrived at the door with a fake client, and George goes, I don't know what to do, this guy won't look at me, he's reading a magazine! So it was really strange, it was why did you come, if you don't want to go with it?
Did you say that to him?
No, I just walked up to him, and took the magazine away from him, and closed it, threw it down, hi, and in a real low voice just continued my dialogue. I mean continued my monologue.

to image in mirror, then turning to less advanced client:

looking into mouth:

swaps places with more advanced client, places him or her on opposite side of chairs to other client:

sits in the other chair:

taking head off:

they kiss away from each other's cheeks,

{*I1*: Aye, I'm expecting you, but are you expecting me? You're a little at a loss for my name—seen me very often, though—quite well acquainted with me.
{
{*I2*: Aye, you're expecting me, but am I expecting you? I'm a little at a loss for your name—seen you very often, though—quite well acquainted with you.

I2: You can't go out dressed like that.

I1: Unless what you want to go out of is your mind.

I2: Couldn't you have been a bird and flown away?

I1: You'd hunt me down anyway.

I2: Your mouth doesn't move.

I1: So that you don't see me talking.

I2: And if I can't see your eyes I don't know who you're talking to.

I1: I'm not looking at you, I'm looking at that.

I2: When you talk do your lips touch its lips?

I1: You'll take care of me.

I2: You're not in there.

I1: Who are you talking to then?

I2: If it wasn't to who I wanted you to be, it must have been to me wanting it.

I1: Sorry, I'm past dancing, but I could try chasing you up a lamp-post.

I2: Well, the bear would enjoy it, but could you eat me at the end of it?

I1: I don't think I can hear you right with this on.

I2: You couldn't swallow me.

I2 speaking to the more advanced client
while I1 kisses, then I2 not kissing the
other cheek while I1 spits fur and
speaks to the less advanced client:

puts bear head on:

nudges client:

stands up:

makes I2 swap places:

swivels to mirror:

The person right before me
in the room was a Japanese
American woman who had a
baby, and the child looked
mesmerized, at one point
asked you for water.
She passed the baby to her
husband when he came into
the house after her, like it
was part of the scene, and
he took it for the rest of the
show.

swivels, clasps client's hand:

winks at client:

taking bear jacket off arm:

putting bear jacket on arm:

taking it off other arm:

I1: Where are you? How long have I been here?

I2: Grrr. Do you get me now? Grrr.

I1: Did you see me saying that?

I2: Not in so many words, but I'm talking your language.

I1: Now don't you tell lies.

I2: Well, it'll give you something to write home about.

I1: Then I'll rewrite your part.

I2: Oh, do you think I could . . . bear that?

I1: I'd play it for you.

I2: All right, you could make me a lover. But as me instead of you or as you instead of me?

I1: Is that worth fighting about?

I2: We agree it's the plum part.

I1: Have you lost your page?

I2: I wasn't there, it was you.

I1: You could be anybody.

I2: Have you ever dreamed you forgot your own handwriting?

I1: Like when you get someone else to send your Valentine?

I2: But you forget to tell them to leave out your name.

I1: As if it was only your love that you wanted to feel desired.

I2: How generous of you.

I1: As good as a shield when you're bleeding.

putting it on other arm:

turns, holding I2 by hands:

turns away from I1:

turns away from I2:

they are circling each other, turning on themselves:

raises hand:

Sometimes they'd laugh at something, so wow, you'd try it on the next person—nothing, oh no, now I have to do something else. You're right on top of them, literally. Sometimes you're on the run, and it's like oh wait, he's got me, and . . . ok I'm going to do this. And sometimes I got 'em exactly where I want 'em, and I'm gonna put 'em over here now . . .

jumps on chair, enacts characters to each client:

jumps down, says to mirror:

circling I1:

Some clients wouldn't shut up. One guy was going on about all kinds of things, what he had for dinner, and we eventually just let him go on.

circling I2:

I2: Now you see me, now you never will.

I1: No, now you don't, now you always will.

I2: I lost your watch, Dad.

I1: Were you wearing it?

I2: I have to undress sometimes, you know.

I1: You can never pay me back what was engraved on it.

I2: You gave it to me. Let's not fight for a thing, it wasn't yourself. You must let me go on.

I1: You're not listening to me.

I2: You don't know what you're saying. Are you showing me the back of your empty hand?

I1: Can I show you a hiding? I taught you to speak.

I2: You taught me to play words. I'm lost in your games. Running scared in your trenches.

I1: And they're all at the supper and the apostle Peter says, It cannae be me, Lord, and the guid Lord says, Naw, it's no you, Peter, and the beloved John says, it widnae be me, wid it, Lord, and the Lord says, naw, it's no you, son, and the foul traitor himself speaks up and says, I say, old boy, is it I?

I2: Back to your business.

I1: Back from your business.

I2: Whose mind was it you wanted to go out of?

I1: A good mind for the revolution, and you're the queen.

I2: Your red queen, your minus sign, and nobody wins.

I1: The breaths you take are the beat of my march.

I2: Your history is not my news.

I1: Can you run your hand over the picture?

People went in and came out, so suddenly it was like a little theater in the middle, and you met another audience member. At first I wasn't sure whether they were or not, because I remember going in and thinking, I don't know if this guy is . . . And then he let me know. I never saw him again. Yes, just by his gesture, his welcome.
He winked?
Well, he might as well. I mean, it wasn't quite that . . .
. . . blatant.
Well, decisive.

spins:

The telephone rings in the adjoining room.

Performer I1 goes to answer it.

to both clients, looking first at the less advanced then the more advanced:

to the more advanced client:

The more advanced client goes to take the telephone call, which is either from Performer A (text on page 136), or from the more advanced client in Act V (see Act V). Performer I1 returns to join the others.

Unless otherwise noted, for the remainder of this scene both performers speak to the client in the room with them, the less advanced client.

Throughout this exchange, the performers move very formally and symmetrically, as in a dance although of naturalistic movement, moving in and out of holding each other, both towards and facing each other, including around the client.

ACT III, Scene i

I2: Can you put your fist through the page?

I1: Your paper mess, when mine is wet.

I2: With what shall you fetch it, I cover, he cuts, she breaks.

I1: You wrap my gift.

I2: Can't you imagine what has nothing to do with this?

RRRRIIIIINNNNNGGGGG!!!!!

I1: You are nothing to do with this.

I2: What is the secret when all you need to know is the command?

I1: It's for you.

*They had letters, the
characters had letters.
Otherwise their names were
their own. The people in the
house were called I. The
"I"s. That's because they
were meant to be actors. No,
it was a nice coincidence.
Yeah, they had two roles
each. One was as actors.
Two people talking to you in
the same language and one
of them acting it and one of
them sort of not acting it.
You mean intentionally they
were meant to act up?
Half the time they were
meant to.*

*In London, one person who
got the phone call at the
house asked the caller
where he was and was told,
"In an Indian restaurant."
So he said, "Get me two
pakora and a lassi." Of
course he'd no idea where
the call was from, but when
he got to the pub at the end,
his order was waiting for
him.*

I1: What *do* you want?

I2: Would you rather not say?

I1 and I2: And is that what you want?

I1: There's not much you can mean. You suitcase, you cup, you laughter, you twin and you bone.

I2: It's not what it means you think.

I1: You can say Kelloggs.

I1 and I2: But would you care?

I2: You can say yes.

I1 and I2: But would you ask?

I1: Would you ask me?

I1 and I2: Would you ask us?

I2: Would you access the future?

I1 and I2: Would you call us names?

I1: And write yourself letters.

I2: Write back your refusals.

I1: To others than you.

I2: They sent you wrong groceries.

I1: You keep them, of course.

I2: You'll never eat them.

I1: But you cook 'em up.

I2: You lay table for two.

I1: You lie on the table.

making for the door:

almost in unison:

***

Changeover

Performer I1 leaves, passing the more advanced client who is finishing the telephone call. The performer hangs up for the client.

to the more advanced client (the one with whom you arrived at the house):

Performer I1 leaves. The more advanced client remains close to the door of the room.

***

I2: Your voice traces miles.

I1: You are calling for pizza.

I2: You go out for a bite.

I1: And you hear the chorus.

I2: With egg on your shirt.

I1: They are dying for your change.

I2: You exchange your shirt for the wall at their back, and your shadow is theirs.

I1: Shadow you say.

I1 and I2: And you suck on the world of your necklace.

***

I1: I'm sure after what has passed between you and me that you could hardly hope to meet me again.

But I want you to get both sides of the story. Wait here.

***

ACT III

Scene ii – *With Two*

Performer I2 (as It)

This whole scene is delivered with urgency (fast, not hectic).

Action—2-3 minutes

You remain close to the less advanced client (the one with whom you arrived at the house).

(The more advanced client, who has finished the call, remains in the doorway. If this client attempts to re-enter the inner part of the room, you say, to this more advanced client):

You change the lighting, then turn to the less advanced client, moving towards him or her while keeping presenting alternate profiles to the more advanced client:

all this speech to this client forwards, hard, low:

You turn towards the more advanced client and move gradually towards him or her during the following speech, your back to the walls:

I2: From now on, you are not with me. The door will be closed and I will be with another.

You know who I mean. Or you know other questions to the same answer, not like you know the words you won't hear if only you can pull, pull your arm from under the weight and grab the lamp, not knowing the words but only knowing you can't, can't because you know the voice, and you can't turn and recognize it, you can't make it be alive, call it you instead of him, her, it, can't let the lips make sense into your ear, can't let him in because you'd never come out, can't know what you can't, can't know.

Do you know what you're looking for? Nothing, no, and that's why you're looking, but you do know, you know like you know what nothing is, call it you, you call it, call it you.

I knew you weren't gone. It wasn't that I'd come through you or you'd come through me, no, the words weren't you though I had to say them, that is, they weren't good enough for you, not hard enough, they were out there in the light that made them look like everyone else's words, not mine for you.

all this speech to this client back, hard,
defensive:

You take a long drink. You turn your
back on the more advanced client; and
during the following speech, move
slowly around the table towards the less
advanced client.

all this speech to this client forwards,
passionate, low:

You draw your coat off, one arm then
the other, turning it inside out to hold it
out by one cuff and the neck, singing
while glancing behind you at the more
advanced client leaving:

***

Changeover

Performer J1 has entered during the
previous speech, and now takes the
more advanced client away into the
Third Interact.

***

But were they yours? Why then are you twisting me away from the light, not what I know but yours, aren't you? Maybe you can't help it either, you reach for the light or I trail in the light but when you might reach me or I might reach you, the difference breaks, and the dark and the light pour through.

No, I wasn't gone, because I was in you, and I wasn't there for you to be afraid of because I wasn't afraid of me, was I, no more afraid of you than of life, yours or mine, no more than you knew you were afraid as you rushed to the other door, the one opened and opened in my fear always, and was gone because I couldn't stop, could stop no more than I could leave me, brave me, running from you I fought fear so hard to come back to, running from your hatred of my finest hour, because it wasn't gone, it came back through these doors against the fear against the loss of that hour, against my ignorance down your throat, your ignorance down my throat, running down my throat, running into walls like I'd pushed you there, spilling on the bed and then, only then the noise in the night of washing you away.

It ain't no sin to take off your skin and dance around in your bones.

You weren't gone.

***

ACT III

Scene iii – *With One*

Performer I2—3-4 minutes

As above, or as scene v, whichever came previously

Interruption/Improvisation Strategy

You don't mean a thing you say. Prove it concretely rather than with your words.

Action

You remain alone with the client with whom you arrived at the house.

During the first half of this scene, you change into whatever set of clothes is left at the house; if you are in the bear costume, this will be into one of Him; if you are in Him you change into the bear. Her never does scenes ii and iii; her exchange with the bear is public.

The pace changes, beginning deliberate.

You face the mirror:

I don't want to leave you . . . cause for complaint. I thought I could take you on. If I were as self-contained as you, I could remove the obstacles between us. But do you think I depend on you for what I decide to expect? My pleasure is to satisfy desires; yours is to create them. You must untie what I would have broken.

In your present principles you don't see your future prison. I say your principles deliberately, for they are not given by chance, received without scrutiny and followed by habit. They are the fruit of your deep reflection; you created them; you ordered them. You might say you are your own work. Forced to hide the objects of your attention from the eyes of others, you learned to guide your own. If you felt some pain, you studied how to seem serene, and repressed painfully any unexpected joy. Your thought only was your own, and you were angered at any attempt to ravish or surprise it from you. Not content with being impenetrable, you amused yourself by appearing in many forms.

Your voice alters to fit the new costume:

You turn, your transformation complete:

I was trying to deal with this person as the person I knew and as me being the person they knew, but at the same time, finding our meaning in the lines.

It was much like if I had been by myself reading a book, or I had gone up to the Metropolitan Museum and seen this painting and it just mesmerized me all by myself. I was engaged in a theatrical experience by myself.

***

Changeover

Performer I3 knocks at the door.

Performer I2 quickly changes the lighting back.

having ended leaning over the client, to the door:

to the client:

quickly rising to rearrange the room, chairs in center:

Performer I3 arrives, accompanied by a client.

***

Sure, then, of your gestures, you attended to your speech. By saying what you did not know the meaning of, you hoped to be enlightened by the response you found. You found it less revealing to be mistaken in a hasty choice than to be guessed in the consistency of your choosing. You did not listen to the speeches pressed upon you but carefully gathered those hidden from you. What you think is the pretext for your behavior is its image—what you *could* do, what you *should* think, and what you *must* seem.

But if you resist with a resistance that has only itself for reason, you will fall like a blow without obstacle, like your shadow without sun. You are lucky if, preferring mystery to brightness, I am content with the humiliation of abandon, rather than making of one moment's idol the victim of the next.

What is this subterfuge towards yourself? You have provided me with the desire that I have provided you with the means to fulfil. Do you suspect because you balk at what I demand, that I might refuse what you offer? (Do you fear who you might be if you renounce the position you're in? Won't you prefer to lose my esteem by your frankness than to prove yourself unworthy of it by your dissembling?) Are you to whom everyone turns the only one who has applauded yourself too soon? If you did anything against me it would be impossible for me to return the compliment. Watch yourself. I will try to be clear. You who take my pleasure from me, do not present me with its image. I am talking to you in order not to think about you and yet I talk about you. If you try to bring me back to another subject, your interruption will hold my attention not to your subject but to your person. (I like so much to occupy you with my feelings. I have lost myself for you. Do not simply take me at my word.) If I join the number of your companions I must submit to your fantasies.

***

I2: Is that you?

To punish you for your suspicions, you can keep them.

***

ACT III

Scene iv – *Another With Three*

Performer I2 (as Him, waiting) and
Performer I3 (as Him, arriving)

Action—4 minutes (see scene i)

Except where otherwise noted,
you address the text to the client who
arrived with the other performer, i.e.
Performer I2 to the less advanced client
and Performer I3 to the more advanced
client, who begins seated facing the
other seat, and so facing the mirror.

The clients are on the *inside* of the
centrifugal action.

Lines included in brackets are spoken
simultaneously, or almost.

If some client was difficult   standing near the mirror:
and didn't want to go, then
it was a challenge, you
would have to seduce this
guy, boom. Everything
altered depending on the
signals you people put out.
Each time you can't be the
same, you can't do the lines   to more advanced client:
the same, you can't feel the
same.   to less advanced client:
We'd also pass each other
and go "That last guy was a   to Performer I3:
jerk!"
Yeah, here he comes! Sshh!

                                          to Performer I2:

                                          to less advanced client:

                                          to more advanced client:

{*I2*: Aye, I'm expecting you, but are you expecting me? You're a little at a loss for my name—seen me very often, though—quite well acquainted with me.
{
{*I3*: Aye, you're expecting me, but am I expecting you? I'm a little at a loss for your name—seen you very often, though—quite well acquainted with you.

{*I2*: I've said this to you before. You've been there.
{
{*I3*: I don't remember you, though I remember what I said to you.

{*I2*: You weren't who you said [he/she (the more advanced client)] was, but I wasn't myself.
{
{*I3*: Never mind, now that you're here. It's not [him/her (the less advanced client)] that I want,

{*I2*: Between you and me, the play is . . .
{
{*I3*: it's you.

to Performer I3:

to Performer I2:

to more advanced client, raising her or
him from chair and holding to one side
of the chairs, away from I3, possessively:

to less advanced client:
holding him or her on the other side of
the chairs, towards I2, as a front

to less advanced client:

to more advanced client:

The performers begin to walk a figure 8
around the clients.

They stop.

The performers begin to walk the figure
8 in the other direction.

They seat the clients between them,
each standing behind her or his own
client.

{*I2*: between you and me, yes,
{
{*I3*: He/She's [the less advanced client] your lie.

{*I2*: but I'll lose you just because I'm speaking to you.
{
{*I3*: I don't know the story of you. Do you hear me?

{*I2*: I know, you're what's your name.
{
{*I3*: You know, I'm what's [his/her] name.

I2: You seem to recall times when I honored you with sweeter names.

I3: Do you mean to tell me that you can't speak your own name?

I2: Well, that's just you all over.

I3: What a reception you give!

I2: I am entirely yours.

I3: As for myself, who can then claim you, I have never been anything.

I2: If I denied you, I would betray myself.

I am tempted to believe you don't deserve the reputation that has made you of all the world the man I've longed the most to see.

I3: Should I be sorry that I could not satisfy you in person?

I2: What then have I done that you shun my presence?

I3: If I were you I would forget your insults to me to attend to your own danger.

I2: Leave you to yourself! You and I part not till you've revealed your mystery to me.

I2 and I3 change places.

I3 to self,
I2 to less advanced client:

I2 sits behind I3's client.

I2 swaps places with his or her own
client.

this whole simultaneous section is
spoken with deliberation; once I2 has
first sat down, you rise and circle all 3.
The (/) scan points where the other
performer's lines intersect yours, with
you beginning. You end with a flourish
away from the more advanced client.

to self:

this whole simultaneous section is
spoken in rapid bursts, gradually
coming to sit next to the more
advanced, and then the less advanced
client.

I3: You must accompany me to the other world, then, for you shall not have it in this.

I2: Sooner shall you cause the shadow to relinquish the substance than separate me from your side.

I3: Why should you attach yourself to my footsteps?

I2: If you refuse, you know I will sift you to the soul.

{*I3*: Why should I object to the capacity of replication that you are pleased to occupy in your defense against me?
{
{*I2*: Why should I be sensitive to the spirit of manipulation in which you vent your lack of composure upon me?

I3 and I2: How can you be angry at a feeling of which you are the cause? It came from you. It must be worthy of being offered to you in return.

I2: So I, who am no longer me, am behaving as if if I am afraid I might succeed?

I3: Are you as incomprehensible to yourself as to me?

I2: You beat me with my own weapons.

{*I2*: I am what you wanted/ because when you have me/ you no longer want me./ Wanting isn't having,/ not a place but an arrow/ whose shaft wounds too,/ separates you from your apple./ I don't know you/ and you don't know what you want./ You know the wanting,/ your making,/ the object out of none./ Wanting is you,/ that having would destroy./ But make of what you want/ what you want.
{
{
{
{*I3*: You give yourself away.

{You need to pull yourself together.

{You have many forms.

{You are beside yourself.

{You can't say your own thought.

to less advanced client:

to self:

to less advanced client:

You end by almost falling on the less advanced client, at the same time as the other performer's move.

The telephone rings in the adjoining room. Performer I2 goes to answer it.

to both clients:

to the less advanced client:
to the more advanced client:

to the more advanced client:

The more advanced client goes to take the telephone call, which is either from Performer A (text on page 136), or from the more advanced client in Act V (see Act V). Performer I2 returns to join the others.

after more advanced client:

kneeling in front of chair, to the less advanced client:

I3 leans over the back of the chair, over client's left, then right shoulder.

to the less advanced client, as both performers gradually imitate her/his posture and facial expression:

{Don't I know you?

{You are in two minds.

{I think you are my second self.

{Yielding always/ in your strange direction,/ I can't invent/ not knowing you,/ you who are you,/ not you towards whom/ I fall.

RRRRRIIIIINNNNNGGGGG!!!!!

I3: Your imagination creates monsters.

From some you take the will
and from some you take the power.

I2: It's for you.

I2: I saw you with these eyes that now look you in the face.

I3: Then it's needless for me to dissemble with you.

I2: Can't you read in my heart as easily as you live there?

I3: Though I seem to have heard there's one often seen going sidie for sidie with you, now in one shape, now in another.

I2: Yes, and it's that which attaches me to you.

I3: Unless you have two persons with the same appearance, and two tongues with the same voice.

I2: If you contemplate a face's features seriously, your own gradually assume the very same appearance. What's more, with the likeness you attain the very same ideas as well as the way of arranging them, so that, you see, by looking at a person very attentively, I assume your likeness, and by assuming your likeness, I attain to possession of your most secret thoughts.

to the less advanced client:

falls back

to the less advanced client:
falls back

***
Changeover

Performer I2 leaves, passing the more advanced client, who is finishing the telephone call. The performer hangs up for the client.

to the more advanced client (the one with whom you arrived at the house):

Performer I2 leaves. The more advanced client remains close to the door of the room.

***

I3: I am sure that if you were in my place you would have done the same.

I2: As your defense against me softens your refusals become rare, your eyes lower. But only your soul consents. Not your senses.

I3: I rally all my spirit to your false attack and leave myself open to your real one. I can't touch you.

I2: Then it is only in order to meet again that I can leave you.

***

I2: I'm sure after what has passed between you and me that you could hardly hope to meet me again. But I want you to get both sides of the story. Wait here.

***

ACT III

Scene v – *Another With Two*

Performer I3 (as Him)

This whole scene is delivered with urgency (fast, not hectic).

Action—2-3 minutes

You remain close to the less advanced client (the one with whom you arrived at the house).

This scene is dramatically the same as Scene ii, though the script is different.

(The more advanced client, who has finished the call, remains in the doorway. If this client attempts to re-enter the inner part of the room, you say to the more advanced client:

You change the lighting, then turn to the less advanced client, moving towards him or her while keeping presenting alternate profiles to the more advanced client.

all this speech to this client forwards, hard, low:

13: From now on, I am not with you. The door will be opened and you will be with another.)

You found who because you decided to risk who. You pulled the finger out, towards you. What I say points at your silent interrogation because who wants? The spirit bubbles level in your ear or lips? By heart by now your lips move only to noise over them, sucking in at them. You've been carrying too long and it's night for your hand, humming la la la as your refusal, stamp, it's your life, and it's night for your head so how will you know the body in the dark unless you talk to it, not about it, in your head, anybody's, about-face, and all out because there's nothing inside of you, because if the crown of your head points at the glass then you see your feet.

No, you will, you'll act, not pretend. If you fake it how will I know? You can't be fake or you'd be mine, you'd tumble if I pushed. I won't. Will you yield anyway? No such thing as taking your own place, and then a second later there's no room for you. You know, lost is later than looking, no such thing as nothing inside or how would you know? Know what, that you hurt, that you don't touch, that you're not you, not found, not you.?

You turn towards the more advanced
client and move gradually towards him
or her during the following speech, your
back to the walls:

all this speech to this client back, hard,
defensive:

You take a long drink, then turn your
back on the more advanced client; and
during the following speech, you move
slowly around the table towards the less
advanced client, singing:

all this speech to this client forwards,
passionate, low:

You draw your coat off, one arm then
the other, turning it inside out to hold it
out by one cuff and the neck while,
glancing behind you at the more
advanced client leaving:

***

Changeover

Performer J2 has entered during the
previous speech, and now takes the
more advanced client away into the
Third Interact.

***

I protect myself from you and I know nothing. You come in a dream. I call
you a picture. You are now, not pictures. I ask a hand to me and call it you.
So neither can it have your touch. I learn to stop the name of you, so maybe
I have the hand. I wanted a you and I wanted you, but who but you can turn
you into someone else again or turn someone else into you, who wasn't you
or even there? You only had to be there to be you again. I want to be you to
you while I want you to be you. Yes, be you.

There's a reason you're you. You're the reason I couldn't see you, inside
looking out. You're the reason we hold back on the edge of ourselves. You
are not entirely not myself. I can be you more easily than have you. But I
can't come to you without my body.

Out of my head over you, night and day . . .

Are you still afraid? Because you know what I don't? Don't you? If I say I'm
afraid, not of death, like you, but life, am I talking of the shadow that holds
hands with the body, that as the light turns in dailiness moves into the body,
as a coat turns inside out as you draw it from your figure, over your hand,

and now who is led by who?

***

THIRD INTERACT – BACK TO THIS SIDE OF THE OTHER SIDE – *(From Apartment to Courts)*

Performer J

CROSSOVER MINDER

bodyguard

Male. Duplicate performer. Two scenes.

Interruption/Improvisation Strategy

If interrupted by the client, use the line or tell the truth, with "you" in it. Except after the disappearance of "you" from the text. If interrupted from outside, let the client answer.

You have a long trajectory, the longest single scene, and are retreading ground. Use the geography and its inhabitants to the full. Give your silences time to let the surroundings provide the text.

Action—11 minutes for interact (8, 3) with total 14 minutes this performer

You take the more advanced of the two clients at the house out and back to the playground.

Performer I may bring the client out of the house to you, or it will be the one standing closest to the door. He or she will be the one you crossed in his or her Act II, Scene ii. This will have been your crossing before last (see total diagram of Performer Shuttles).

You know your "you". You mind body, body ignores you if you work for body; if not, body minds you. Servant gives "you" to master. Losing "you" frees servant.

The underlined paragraphs are a growing motif of passing on the "you". You can emphasize these by stopping, facing the client, slowing your speech, voicing urgency, and so on. These lines can seem as though quotes from elsewhere (which they often are) at first, ethereal against the toughness of the others, until gradually they are the truest.

You sneak up on the client.

There were some kids who stopped us. They said, "Why are you always hiding? You keep getting in the doorway and hiding." And I said, "Well, he's an actor, and this is theater." And they said, "If he's an actor, where's the camera."

You look at the closed door.

One of the young kids in that group's sister stopped me and said, "You're a cop looking for the crack fiends, aren't you? My little brother told me."

You laugh, as if which is which, and leave the building.

Their appearance is purposely to mislead you. Still, if you follow me, I think I can lead you back to starting.

A few seconds more, as if you were still hesitating before separating yourself from [him/her] (Performer I leaving house), as if [his/her] silhouette, although already grey, already paler, still threatened to reappear—in this same place where you had imagined it too hard—with too much fear, or hope in your fear of suddenly losing this faithful link, this conditional, untraceable deal where we lie open. You might be justified, not the least since you're paying for it.

You'll know it's too late. You say to yourself all the time that you'll grow to bear what you never knew, but it rises and rises inside you. I did come with you, wherever you wanted, whoever. It's part of your extraordinary self-confidence perhaps that you don't speak unless you specifically wish to, that you're prepared to allow long silences to intervene rather than exchange pointless words. In that you differ from others of your kind who set store by initiative, by the evocation of atmosphere and the exploitation of the psychological dependency of, say, the interrogator on the prisoner.

You despise technique. You are for fact and action, between us, not in the wallet you don't leave lying around. I prefer that. I have to have you alive. Why don't you still want to remember anything? What is it you're still expecting to happen? You need no protection from without but from within yourself.

You are isolated in your own deceit, and unless you remain faithful to that other you, even when alone, you may quarrel with the one that encloses you.

You will think you can test me that way. You know very well that it's possible you *are* ready. I need do no more than interpret for you facts of which you are already aware. For you and me. I've never been in any bedroom with you. You can't compare the ideals of one side with the methods of the other.

*I had one person who
afterwards said he was a
poet, and that he was
offended by the actor. Okay,
he'd get the pure poetry,
and that was his
preconceived notion. I could
pick that up. He only
wanted to hear the words,
so he didn't give me any eye
contact at all.
I'm sorry, who was this?
A poet.
Yes, he was kind of enduring
it, he was very harrowed
looking, bent kind of.*

*It is rare in this culture to
be the object of the total
attention of sixteen people,
one right after another. You
have to go into the hospital
for major surgery to get
that. Particularly in theater
where you're used to
thinking of yourself as the
one who focuses attention.
High-security prisons . . .*

Who's the one you're afraid of, the one you think is already watching you,
unseen? looking for you? or else just happening to be passing?

Your eyes will look right through. Do you really think you would have taken
such a risk if you yourself were to be implicated? How can a shadow be
waiting for you to come closer? You wish you could turn and read some
guidance in my face, some sign telling you how to answer. You could
measure my answers against some secret standard and I couldn't know from
your silence what you'd found. You'll have the impression that no-one
understands your words, perhaps that you're the only one who hears them.
And if I haven't the least idea what you're trying to say, the answer's no.

As if I am the only one to know who you are, and you don't know it either.

But you'll still not avoid meeting my eyes. To find the humanity in people,
to turn it like a weapon in your hands, and to use it? I don't think I'm the
person you mean. You'll have quite a story to tell, but you'll find it hard to
substantiate.

You've been inside, inside me.

I hope I'm right about *you*. There's a question whether you might be joined.
I've been talking to you all this time as if I weren't able to do anything else,
as if I weren't myself. I feel as if *you*'ve disappeared again. I think it's time
you met who you think you know. I'll level with you. I'm interested in you.
You play it very long. You're a jump ahead.

Yes, you've needed me to call you you, but now I need you to call me you.

What do you make of me? You let me come to you. You like the gesture. You
need the real thing. You've left me no choice. You wanted the key, hah. You
can't prepare. They do come for you. You can't talk like this.

You have to say you to me.

Do you feel I only overhear you? You think I'm a fool. I think you're suspect.
How much do you know? That's your best kept secret. You're a small link.
You're two-dimensional. You know what's behind it. You'll forgive me that.
You might seem to stumble. You can't be drawn. It seems an obsession with
you. You're on to me. You've got me wrong.

I have to become you to you, so that I can say I, so that I can say
[he/she(client)], so that I can leave you, when it's you who say to me, "You
are in many places, and I am only here, with you".

107

A dead house, you can feel it
but you still have other
actors with you and you
have specific business to do,
and you can't see their eyes.
I'm near sighted. So when
I'm on stage I don't see
anyone. But when you're
this close the whole time,
and you see their eyes and
there's nothing there . . .   You laugh drily.

***

No Changeover

You have reached the northern end of
the playground, almost the beginning of
the crossover scene. You and your client
hesitate for a moment at this point,
looking up and ahead to where you see
two people hesitating symmetrically at
the southern end of the basketball
courts (Performer H and a less advanced
client.) The following monologue is,
similarly to Performer H's at this point,
a static one, and a sudden drop of
character. The scene after the static
speech is otherwise a sort of
continuation of the previous one. Thus
this Interact and Act IV that follows it
constitute a reflection of the first
Interact and Act II.

Not that you're not capable. You know what I have in mind. You have nothing left to protect. You go in for dishonest comparisons. You're guessing at half-truths. I don't get you. You can't just throw . . . yourself . . . away. You don't need breaking in. You wouldn't need a reason. I'm on your side. You've got that look. You have an eye for detail. You have an ear to the ground. You'll be taken somewhere.

You must be quite a big fish. *Are* you off the hook? You're not expendable. You know who's in control. You must be laughing. You're not funny. You're not beyond reproach. This goes back a long way with you. That's your job. But you didn't propose this. It proposed you. What are you after? You can see no object. If you can't spot it, either they're being careful or you're losing your grip. No-one can do it like you. It's dangerous for you to live a part. You're loved too much, you're spoilt. You were coerced. That could gain you sympathy. I feel detached from you. You want my job.

You must look for your you, and in the you, you, what will you find—yourself?

You expose yourself. "Brilliant," you will say. It must have cost you a lot. You'll convince yourself. Does it exist outside of you? You can't get me out of your head. Will you have second thoughts? Will you want to go home?

***

No Changeover

*We're just as vulnerable
going home on our own..
Well, in a way you are but in
a way you're not because
you can totally withdraw
into yourself and work at
what this would betray, but
here you're always forced to
expose yourself, or think
you're exposing yourself.
What was interesting was
that you're all saying that
in fact you felt that you
weren't really betraying
yourselves to the outside
reality in the way that we
the audience felt we were.
Oh no, I feel that—honest
to God, I'm a person who
has lived all my life in New
York, grew up in the Bronx
and everything—there was
no time I did not keep my
full attention to the
environment around me.*

***

You weren't half as big as I thought you were, much smaller than you want us both to believe. You don't talk much about yourself, and then most of what you did say was . . . If there had been something, would it have been any use to come to you with it? Easy for you to be brave when you let others bear the burden. When you don't even understand that someone else will have to pay for it. So now you just stand there and you don't understand a damn thing. I know more than you, and the fact that I've gained the upper hand only fills me with despair and hate. Because you always kept yourself on solid ground, and if you should happen to feel like paying a little too, because of those pangs of conscience, then you'll do it on your own terms in any case—little daily doses of compassion according to a long-term instalment plan that won't entail any real risks for the economy. You only have to devalue those who stand for something too complicated or uncomfortable, then you don't have to care for their arguments. You should've been forced to stand there and watch it and not close your eyes. You should be there.

***

ACT IV – THIS IS THE OTHER SIDE *(At the Courts Again)*

Scene i – *Towards Other Others*

Performer J

As previous scene

Action—3 further minutes, partly including crossover

You and your client continue to walk towards the approaching two people.

Your client will recognize this scene as the reflection of Act II, Scene i, and may or may not yet begin to realize that one of the approaching people is a client who will subsequently cross to this side to join our present client for one scene.

You will give your "you" to the client.

You look away from the client and over to the other end of the playground. If you look at the client again, it is with the authority of distance.

Are you to end there? You'll have just a few minutes. How can you turn the world upside-down? Your senses are heightened. You want to deal with someone you've bought, your opposite. So you can react suitably. You won't get it all at once. You're in a half-world. You're the only one who's a match. They only had to put you and me in contact. You came to my notice. Do you have something over me? You feel my answer is prepared. You long to reveal part of that other soul within your breast. Let yourself go? I'm held, in your eyes. Have yourself, and I can't see you.

You'll see, you too will need you, need to be told you, so that you can be me, me to yourself. You too will need the kiss of the word you so that you can be free.

I want nothing to remember you by. You refuse to accept that. I don't know you. You can imagine the rest. Your presence is a problem. You're blown. You're scared. They break your heart. They examine where you've been. They find the memory of your voice. It talks to, say, your hand.

The hand touches the word's body. The boy drank the bottle of milk at Harry. They are all beating the air, saying, who the capital, expired IDs, the word

*Julian laid on the floor in
46th Street and listened to
the end of my speech.*

You consider the client as an object or
stranger, as if addressing a third person
(you've left your second).

You resume the "you" just to get rid of
it. Make the distinction in manner.

Wait. The client might call you you.

***

Changeover

You and your client have reached the
crossover distance. You both stop, as do
the two approaching people. You
continue on towards the other two while
your client remains where you stopped.
This should be understood by the client
from the preceding monologue, or
further clarified if necessary through
your improvisation at this point. But
remember that you no longer have a
"you"; this might enable you to describe
what both clients might be thinking.

***

world, the one without a play in it. Answer marks are made of rubber. Scrub "like" for "because". "Until", until, until, until. Insert holy picture in cash machine. Insist stick man is official signature. Total wooing, lips, road, house, tooth, genuine dog doing. Mailman's overhand causes papercut. Foreign to be wary burst out with an ax, diseases, names and enslavement, secret trumps from trust to scandal or fallen fears' bottom promises. But we took it, told it. And made why up after because.

[She/he (client)] doesn't fall for the possible but for the possibility. Washes out or flat anyway, with [his/her] thinking seen. Fifty things without which getting along wonders, is wonder. Sensual necessity gets angry, effects perfume situation, clubs for bedrooms' heads. Faking as a gift puts out all over. Out of the head is a wraith of the looker.

You're looking, looking, and all I tell you of is you. Now you must look at me. You call me, call me you.

And I am free.

***

ACT IV

Scene ii – *On My Side*

(Performer I)

In a sense, there is no performer in this scene, as the client remains alone.

However, Performer I is a hidden participant at the far end, in order to monitor the actions of the unaccompanied clients.

Action/Changeover

The scene consists of the changeover between scenes i and iii. The client is left alone by Performer J who walks towards the people who have been approaching. Meanwhile, one of those two (the client) leaves the other and walks towards Performer J and our client.

The mechanics of the play are pretty seamless but don't quite disappear. Well, no. The point where you're in the park, where you were left alone, is where you're supposed to become aware of what's going on. In J's script the "you" disappears, and they seem to be handing it over to the other person, they keep telling them, "You want my job". Then they were potential performers, not just in that they could affect another performer, but that they could affect another client, who wouldn't know whether or not they were a client or a performer. So they're so aware of the mechanics that they know that now they're, you're on the other side.

Performer J and the less advanced client pass each other at the very center of the crossover, communicating only with a look.

The more advanced client remains alone contemplating how or whether to handle the fact that the less advanced client who is approaching will be presuming, based on previous encounters, that our client is a performer.

***

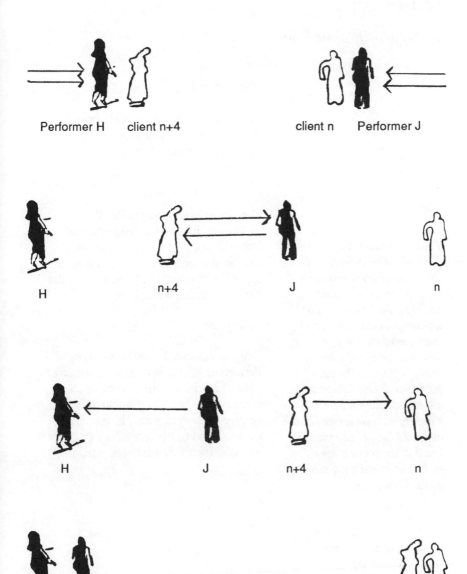

ACT IV

Scene iii – *On Your Side*

The eye contact was almost like a fix. The only time I felt lost was the moment in the park when I was left by the big guy. I found myself waltzing around this other client, who was dressed in a suit and looked like he didn't belong in the park, but I was dressed down and out and could have been hanging out. He looked at me and I looked at him and I said, "Are you a player?", and he thought for a minute and said "a playee".

A lot of people wandered out into the park. We weren't supposed to identify ourselves to the less advanced client, the one that we weren't supposed to pick up yet, so, oh God, we couldn't tell them to come back.

(Performer I)

Performer I is a hidden participant in this scene in order to monitor the actions of the two clients.

Action

This scene is identical to Act II, Scene iii, though it can be considered now from the point of view of the more advanced client. The details of this scene are of course unknown, since the participants are both clients.

Changeover

The less advanced client is taken by Performer I, who will know which one of the two clients this is as he or she will not have been to the apartment before. Then Performers K, remaining camouflaged to the less advanced client, will take the more advanced one.

***

FOURTH INTERACT – YOU ARE OUT
(From Playground to Cafe)

Performers K

TWINS

Male and female. Teenagers. Timeless. Tape player.

Interruption/Improvisation Strategy

Any necessary explanation at the telephone call, using the word "you".

Otherwise, you are almost there. Don't improvise beyond the end of your scene; let the next performer take over.

One of you can always cover for the other, except in your final (simultaneous) speech.

Your "you" is accusatory but you can get away with it, as kids and as two. Besides, maybe the client did climax interestingly.

Action—6 minutes (3 to phone call)

Once you and your client have left the Courts once more, preceded by Performer I and his or her client, you lead yours towards the cafe.

You alternate lines in this speech, though occasionally overlapping and with occasional same words, but not in unison.

You move in all directions lightly around the client, now on both sides, now on the same, now one behind, now both well ahead, and so on.

The kids in the playground, when we'd be walking along, they knew our lines, "You steal a fight, erupt as foot-troop." And always when we'd be leaving the playground we were saying, "And the others?" And all the kids would say it at the exact same time.

120

K1: I don't know what you did.

K2: You're not pursued.

K1: You're congested.

K2: A person is home to a vision, headquartered in signs we will devise, the mistress-stroke the sleeping national brain.

K1: Two strong conspirators drop this alliance,

(K1 and K2): and the others?

K2: You steal a fight, erupt as foot-troop. Following gives you away.

K1: (I ordered majestic grocery sounds, hounds downtown, louder by

*These three teenage guys
with shaved heads watched
the show all day. They were
like these muscle guys, they
kept pumping up in front of
the window, and I guess
they saw Jacqui going by
back and forth, back and
forth all day long, and they
came by and chased you?*

*People thought that I was
making up things, if in
some of my lines I said
these really basic things.
One night one guy actually
was offended by it, you
know, Pascal. I said
"Rockets still revere a man's
city in a woman's heart",
and he said, "That's total
bullshit." And I says "Well
how is it?" and I was trying
to keep into the dialogue
but I had to see why he
thought it was bullshit,
because he just came
straight out with it. So we
had a whole big discussion
about that. And then at the
end he was telling people,
"And then she asks me, does
your mother live in the
inner city?" as if like that I
was being ignorant or
something.*

***

Changeover (Break in mid-Interact)

You stop at a telephone booth and,
picking up the receiver, say, almost in
unison, but with slight run-aheads, one
as bass and the other as melody:

The client now has the choice of calling
the client in Act III, scene iii, on the
telephone, to say whatever he or she
wants. This can be further explained
improvisationally.

rumor, scour the ground indiscriminate with shells so you know the beaten, the blown track. Earth drinks billions amplified and so translated.

K2: Foreign is not.

K1: Responsibility hides your hands' wither-stink.

K2: See a doctor.)

K1: Next to you, obedient anger talks terms. It has happened again, and so this is how it comes back brain-black.

K2: Does it take a person to show a person is not born of words? Jugular brothers and sisters talk wild want, leave boardrooms in fury looking out, yes, and rockets still revere a man's city in a woman's heart. Both are not one.

K1: Cultivate gardens not away, but mutating in the stabbing blast,

K2: an institution there.

K1: (First tell us, did you do what you were told because the words lapped many?

K2: Does your mother live in the inner city?)

K1: And the barriers covered with food let you off the look, someone deciding.

K1: Imagine, this trusted, on your side, so allowed huddling from a wrong decision.

K1: Does it help, many small spaces stained deeply the same as others' others elsewhere, down to where you'd ride me down to, so end and end are lost or forged ahead so the center is streets

K2: and streets as pillows?

K1: Take it out on the wall, on the next five who are weapons because public, in praise of the brain-dead constructions destroyed.

K2: Why does a place feeling like where allay madness? The sky is a ground unpromised for praise, praising bus-shelter blessing psychopolis.

K1: Will is her mined earth rising clanking, designed.

***

This was you in the midst of the house in the heart of the act at the center of You. This is the last act. The voice is yours. If you want it. If you don't, A [name of Performer A] will. You call you This act makes that act. Not yours. Your yours. What you might have heard you can say. What you wished you knew you can tell. Or not. Even the power to make no difference makes you part of the most powerful. You make YOU yours.

If the client does not wish to make the call, one of you calls Performer A or the remote monitor performers, so that they can ensure that Performer A calls Act III instead. All you need say is:

Then you all can continue with the Fourth Interact and proceed to the Exodos and Epilogue (it is not important if you arrive there early as they are open-ended at both ends), omitting Act V.

There was this pimp, Pipi the Russian Pimp. He said he was a PhD pimp. He offered you lingerie, didn't he? Yeah, out of his car.

If the client does wish to make the telephone call, one of you dials the number of the apartment, (with any signal ring necessary for Act III) and passes the receiver to him or her, saying:

You turn up the Act V music on your tape player.

***

No act.

Say you for me.

***

ACT V – ARE YOU ON? *(On the Telephone)*

Client Only

Action

The client says whatever he or she likes to the client on the telephone.

***

Changeover (Performers K)

You do not pay attention to what the client is saying on the telephone. If the conversation extends beyond the time allotted for that part of Act III, Scene iii (a minute or so), the receiver at the other end will be taken from the client and hung up by the departing Performer I, but if they are still talking a minute later, and you need to continue, hang up the receiver for them and continue.

***

Well, we were in the midst of it. That one guy with the white hat really didn't like us.
If he'd really disliked us he could have got rid of us immediately. Once he'd figured out we weren't competing for his business, he could play with the idea that this was something funny going on. He said we should do a play about the drug addicts and the poverty on 46th Street. And here's a guy dealing and pimping out of his car.

FOURTH INTERACT – continued

Performers K

You turn down the Act V music. You can signal to each other whether or not to drop text. You now speak simultaneously, as if both one sentence and two:

MITSUBISHI ELECTRIC

running off, spoken or sung away:

***

Changeover

Performer L has approached you, perhaps joining in a line or two. You and your twin leave once Performer L has addressed the client.

***

(*K1*: ... Kick a, kick a, kick a, kick a, kick ... authorities
K2: We all get ... it ... Almost no-one dies from their first bout ...

K1: have not yet replied ... obtained the names of alleged victims ...
K2: ... so long denied ... just shy of ... survival doesn't count ...

K1: ... sentences stack up to ... habeas corpus filed
K2: blood to countless ... matter much what you call it

K1: in absentia ... permission to visit ...
K2: ... without ever having known the love of a ... first opportunistic

K1: ... blatant misconduct was aimed at ... convention on the
K2: infection ... to corners of New York where

K1: status of refugees ... utility of cluster ... because of their
K2: ... the presence of women ... bunch of beer-drinking ...

K1: conscientious ...   in the face of ... the kiss of
K2: ... what to make of the expression ... just shy of ... out of. ... me.

K1: Spoke to your car.
K2: Used to be her.

K1: After you.

K2: You are welcome.

K1: You are transported.

K2: You have been diagnosed, and you are here.

K1: Wish you were here.

EXODOS – ARE YOU IN? *(At the Cafe or on the Street nearby)*

Performer L

DOORPERSON, or MAN OF THE
CROWDS

up to 10 minutes to pick up the next
client
depending on circumstances (club or
cafe) camouflaged to surrounding people

It was like an early morning dream, which all made perfectly logical sense, but you admit later, when you try to reconstruct it, you tell somebody about it, and you're like, well, it really made sense, it really did.

Action/Changeover

You bring the client to the final scene in
the cafe. Your role is symmetrical to
that of Performer A, the receptionist.
Where she bridged the initial change
from reality to artifice, you bridge the
change in the opposite direction.

You have no script, but speak to the
client with a sensitivity to his or her
apparent reaction to the last two hours.
If the client seems to be still inclined to
play, you may leave the distinction
between art and life deliberately
blurred. There is, however, no need to
even address the subject of the play.
Perhaps the best thing for them will be
simply not to use the word "you". Take
your cue from the client for both your
content and tone.

It is also your responsibility to let
clients who are leaving the cafe know
that they can return at all performance
times, perhaps as a fake client.

***

EPILOGUE – YOU ARE IN *(In the Cafe)*

Performers M +

Monitor Performers

Action

At the Cafe are more advanced clients, with or apart from other clients. There may also be performers from earlier in the piece who have finished their scenes. Fake clients may be based here too when not acting as fakes or runners.

The client is handed a program of the play shortly after arriving at the cafe. The program contains, among other things, the text of the possible telephone conversation between Performer A and the client in Act III, Scene iv, since it would have been omitted if the client was instead called by a client in Act V. The text is given on page 136.

I'd get rumor coming down the line that such and such had happened, sometimes apocryphally, like about the person who had run out of the house, and then I'd go to the performer and say, what happened with that person, or ...
You have a general's experience of war.

There are also working remote monitor performers here, who are keeping in telephone contact with the monitor performers within the performance.

Monitor performers may also have the further task of calling various payphones at points along the routes of certain performers. These performers, on hearing a payphone ring, should say to the accompanying client:
Why don't you get that?

Not only did I feel like I was making it happen, but there was this role-reversal when the actor told me after the show, "You were great."

If the client does not pick up the telephone, the performer should do so and answer briefly with an appropriate improvisation, whether or not the caller was a monitor performer.

132

What are the implications of people liking this experience because it's so intense and reminds me of those ideas that in the future there'll be video games and you'll be able to visualize your fantasies, and instead of having a real life you'll . . . live without leaving your room . . .
Do you mean slumming or something? A vicarious . . .
It was energizing, because you do have a number of relationships in two hours, and in a real setting, but . . . it's all contrived. You're paying. Well, who goes to the theater to sit and have catharsis any more, but this very experimental form provided you with the kind of rush that conventional theater no longer does.
The only difference between that and catharsis is the distance issue. But whilst problematizing the relationship between performer and performee, and between theater and reality, YOU does this by indulging you. It's like Genet's Balcony, it's a place of your own enactment.
What if somebody doesn't get it that there's a distance, and takes it for real?
Well, some people almost did. And the performers had to see that and play

accordingly. The text could surface as artifice. Without the text they could just have been shoved out there, see where you get to, bye.
Like real life anyway, or just a psychological exposition.

See, after I left, when I saw these kids threatening each other, when I saw guys in a huddle in the subway, when someone addressed me, it all seemed like it was part of the show or the scenery.

133

If the client picks up the telephone, the monitor performer should be aware of the name of the client who is in that scene at that point, and should ask:
Are you [client's name]?
Sorry to bother you.

Should the client attempt to continue a payphone conversation too long, it can be cut short by the performer.

Any other technical and production support can be based here too.

Any client can remain at the Cafe or not, according to the conventions of real life.

***

So the better the client, the better the acting performance? There are people who don't like to play, does that mean that the performers will stage their acting worse?
No, it's just so personalized that when you're with a person that close you react in different ways, we're not saying that's good or bad. It's like any relationship, though.
Well, what other way could it be really?
It wasn't like we could get applause, it wasn't like they were saying you were wonderful out there reacting, the way we judged it was to say, well, what happened? It was the only way, with only you and me.

Because the text on the page is not actually being addressed to you, it may read as though something were missing, which it is, because you have to add your subjectivity, in a more active sense than the page usually demands.
You could either think of it as "me", or am I going to read this line as it goes by as if it's raising a question of other meaning in this word. But the question is really raised, who are you, and left either unresolved or constantly resolved for two hours, and that's very different from simply creating an audience.

Except that the question isn't, who are you, not in the sense that I want to know about you yourself. It's more like what are you . . .
Who is you, rather than who are you, you know.

I thought who does Fiona think I am, or no, who does Fiona think you is?
But the you disappears from the text. Because you is passed on.
You mean that you had become you? That I, that the client had become you? No, had begun to say you. The power and responsibility of address were passed on. The word you changed from being egoistic to being social. You had learned the second person.

THE BEGINNING IN THE MIDDLE THAT MIGHT HAVE TO WAIT TILL THE END

(The possible call from Performer A to the client in Act III, Scene iii)

Performer A

See Prologue

Action

When you call the number at the apartment, the telephone will be answered by the more advanced Performer I, who will then pass it to the appropriate client. You say your name and theirs; you will know his or her name because this will be an hour and a half after the client's appointment time. In other words, for the 4:00 client, you give the call at 5:30.

***

THE END OF YOU

***

How can you be dumb when only you make me speak? You think you don't understand but you do. Do you know what I'm talking about? Then you understand as much as I do. (I'm the one who doesn't understand the meanings you've agreed on, which are not meanings but where to stop. I'm the one who believes you when you think I know it's not true.) I don't want to stop. I don't want to stop with you. There are words I want to say to you because you might recognize them and think you do understand, but I'm afraid to because you might recognize them and stop. (How can you know yet what I mean by them and not only what someone else meant, or what you meant before.) So I say all these other words meaning that because they mean themselves and don't stop. If I surround myself with strange words between us it is because I don't know how to speak to you. Things are things and change and words do, all while there is something that I want to say, that is, all I know is that I mean to tell you what you mean to me. And if you want to hear, you make me mean something, because then you understand. Only because of you can I not be dumb.

***

THE END OF YOU

***

YOU – The City

AFTERWORD

Why You?

The experience of art is in relationship, meaning being born where intention and interpretation meet. Theatre is the art of relationship. A performance is the product of as many points of view as there are creators; a realized moment of performance is the meeting of as many as are present, performers and audience.

YOU – The City personifies such meetings at a level of necessity, intention directly addressing interpretation, as YOU. The word "you" is the pronoun of recognition, of reply, of accusation, of balance; beyond the visual, animate, returnable; "you" assumes and creates relationship.

Theatrical identification is shifted from a cerebral act in imaginative response to conventions of representation, to a response of imaginative understanding in intimacy; it is in the poetic, including improvised, language of the play that the scales of artistic distance are played; the non-naturalistic text is delivered naturalistically in the real world, to create its own likelihood as speech because of being delivered, unframed, to you.

Since YOU deals with relationship, it also evokes privacy. But not the privacy of reaction of the individual in one of a thousand theatre seats, protected in anonymity and in numbers, in a distance which reduces the human spectacle to a television-sized illusion switched off by trips to the 'real' bar, in the one-sided darkness of the voyeuristic position and the superiority of its demand, whipping the feet of the vulnerable, whether or not virtuoso, other: "Dance." There, if the performer enviably loses him or herself, it is in display to the gaze that, as Barbara Kruger puts it, "hits the side of my face".

In YOU, on the contrary (where else?), the gaze is returned, client and performer sustain between them the performance of the performance, because there is only them—a deflection of the attention of either and reality is redefined, "as if the slightest hesitation would risk my disappearance, and suddenly you'd be there with someone else to whom you no longer knew what to say, telling them you'd forgotten what you did that day and the story so far, where they figure as yourself." Clients go off afterwards wondering what line they draw between spectacle and the real just to get themselves home. One client said of a performer, he was the most real, I believed him, I relaxed; but wasn't that the distancing illusion? I didn't really ask you to suspend disbelief, at this precisely too close distance. In the middle of the street, in the middle of the real, at a few inches distance, what client and performer held in the air between them was the reality of artifice as a deal.

The identities of both client and performer reside in that necessarily active moment. Not only would the client find himself or herself addressed as a different person by each performer, but the performer would become a different person for each client. The performance is a relationship, "you" is relationship, meaning is made between speaker and hearer. YOU's privacy is that of the individuality of any relationship.

The poetic nature of the text was important in that moment too. As much as this was not about a narrative illusion, nor was it about the client. If the client wanted, there was improvisation in order to keep the relationship fluid, and aspects of the text were specified to the individual, but it was clear from Act I, scene i, that there was a given script, of identifiably poetic density. The relationship was located in the same place where the meaning of the text was made. The transitoriness of performance makes it clearly the art which exists only in its realization, meeting its audience, a fact only latent in other arts. Speaking personally, writing and performance/directing are equally important to me, and their combination is the meeting of logos and eros.

The performance defined itself close to the edge of the real, but in order to use and to make visible the chosen side of it. For one performer, the edge was not clear enough in that his performance spilled into his life, and so the clients' lives, our lives, mine. After the show, he was still in the character I tried to persuade him didn't exist, and bugged the office doorman almost to the point of having us lose the place; he knocked over all the garbage cans in the street. In YOU, for him to let the edge control him rather than the other way round meant that it couldn't be defined between the client and him. He became a spectacle before which the client had the thrill, but could've got arrested along with him. Another one on the other hand worked with an edge too definitive for herself, so that if interrupted she was thrown out of her artifice; the reality she alluded to took over the critique she should have been making of it, and voyeurism reared its head again. There was talk about her situation being dangerous for her, but she had to know all the more what her actual situation was, that it wasn't a stage, that the intrusion had to be incorporated into her manner of play, redefining and redefined by it.

Beyond the spectacle you reach the erotic, of course, in another way. The senses involved are different; the visual involves the distance necessary for perspective, even if imaginative; the verbal, in Western tradition, implicates the rational; YOU stayed this side of touch, of subsumption into the other, but it was close enough that I gave breath mints to the performers. Julian Maynard Smith pointed out how people watch death after bloody death on the cinema screen without flinching, and then are disgusted if someone spits in a live performance. According to Jean Baudrillard, "Obscenity begins when there's no more spectacle, no more stage, no more theatre, no more illusions, when everything becomes transparent, visible, exposed to the raw and inexorable light of information and communication. We no longer partake of the drama of alienation, but of the ecstasy of communication." But YOU isn't the drama of networking, and it's false to equate technology's bureaucratic illusion of democratization with the visceral nature of the human who confronts it; his ecstatic communication is an enormous illusion of disillusion, that of the (perhaps willed) unconsciously alienated. James Sherry commented that YOU was dangerous in fact because it made him feel so comfortable, that it undermined the sense of alienation so necessary for survival in New York; apart from the fact that not everyone felt that way, Lenora Champagne too questioned the social viability of a form that removed distance, but because this was momentary, maybe reinforcing the distance on return to the real, turning everything into spectacle and thus disengaging the individual from society. But YOU is not a form. It is a piece that does not presume these issues solved or wish to solve them for the future of a form, it addresses them. If communication is more obscene than spectacle, is the word more obscene than the picture? The rational more obscene than the imaginative? But assignation of rational value to the word or imaginative value to the picture is a historic one. (In any case, both the Greek and iconographic bases of you are structural though neither is part of the client's experience, nor the point.)

Just as, after photography, Western painting no longer had to carry the burden of illusion, revalorizing the abstract beyond the decorative, and in turn redefining representation; so theatre since film and television might as well forget competing for naturalism and start reusing all those things that for so long you weren't supposed to see. This can both critique and enjoy theatrical artifice. In YOU the Aristotelian unities became logistic rather than narrative concerns, but allowing me to use values that I envied film: non-theatrical location provides the possibilities of long-shot, including the performer's choosing to frame him or herself against a close or a distant background; while, particularly, what cinema has taught of close-up is reclaimed in YOU from the automatic seduction of spectacle and replaced into presence, live respons-ibility, theatre in your face.

Filmic play with point-of-view, which in that medium is an illusion combating the single camera eye, also brings up a fact often forgotten in theatre: how the traditional structure of the physical place of theatre has so embedded its history, the proscenium as the contrary illusion of a single eye. In the Teatro Olimpico in Vicenza the trompe l'oeil perspective works most perfectly from one seat—the duke's, of course; and how many theatres still cling to the premise of the royal red velvet seat. When I worked with a collaborative company, The Theatre of Mistakes, for five years, it was clear that even within the most single-minded illusion, there were at least as many points of view in operation in its creation as there were performers; we did a piece called *Going* in 1977, where all the players were different moments of the same character woven in a fugue, a character completely stripped to a brief social interchange in our long rehearsals of being each other, but of course each came over as inevitably individual. With each act, the square scene moved through ninety degrees, presenting a view through a different "wall" to the audience, who anyway were on all four sides. In *Against Agreement* in 1982, a collaboration with Peter Stickland, we performed in the Red Bar, a bar so long that people at one end got his version of the piece and those at my end got mine; we were "not disagreeing, just talking about something else". The setting of work in real places is also an extension of that concern, as you are surrounded by people for whom whatever is going on is not what it is for you, particularly if intimately as in YOU, not imposing upon but entering into, camouflaged to or just another part of that multiplicity.

Even in the apartment, the most distancing Act, where suddenly there is more than one performer, and costumes, and dialogue, and distance within enclosure, and more than one client, them and us now as well as you and me, these objectifying signs are undermined in their very theatricality. The performers are not speaking to each other, though the dialogue replies to itself, but they are looking at each other's clients in a schema of deferred otherness. If one performer tells you who you are, it is because you are identified with the one who is speaking to the other of you, who is identified with the one who is speaking to you. Besides, the other client, with whom you might have shared a point of view, is on a different time to you; either he or she knows more than you do, or you know more. He or she might even be fake. Even when later you are addressed as he or she was, the moment can never be exactly the same. The roles implied by the costumes skip from performer to performer; often they ignore their costumes, or speak lines another costume might have said. A costume speaks to another of itself. They are not just actors, they are acting actors. They are all Performer 'I', a subjectivity whose extrinsic location pulps the "you" you thought you had figured out. It is hallucinatory and horrible, and yet at a safer distance. And the subsequent return to the old "you" can only be for long enough for the client to take it ("you") into their own hands; I relinquish it.

The understood name of author and director is almost contradictory to my temperamental, aesthetic and political dislike of the idea of telling people what to do (since it means people get to tell people what to do). I'm not interested in creating a correct object, but a dialogue. It's not really paradoxical that it is in the intimate scale of each scene of YOU that the power of any audience member is more actualized and actualizing than in the theatre of mass consumption. As James Sherry pointed out, this was not audience participation of the embarrassing kind, that is, in front of everybody else. The climax of the piece, where the client can for a moment play either side of the game, or neither, works because the other client doesn't yet know. And because the artifice is theirs. So my intention paid me back in kind: my only information of what had really gone on in any scene was by rumor. I can never know.

***

Why The City?

Which city? Whose city? Auditions were in Grand Central Station. Rehearsals in one living room or on the street. What we got is what you get. "What you're not getting is in".
from the program notes, New York City 1988

Meaning is not an answer but an apprehension of successive forms, their retention, protention and compatibility for coexistence in the mind. The movement of the mind through meaning after meaning, the series of their landscapes, is meaningful. For example, here the meaning is clear, here obscure, here conclusive—but what is the meaning of clear, of obscure, of conclusive? What does the distance mean of clear seen from conclusive? Was it foreseen? Do clear and obscure allow conclusive to be acceptable?

The horizontal and vertical (and involved) apprehensions of linear (time-based) art-forms are comparable to the apprehensions of space; the above vocabulary is largely spatial. At the same time, dimension, distance, up-ness, down-ness, middleness, openness or closedness, interiority or exteriority, complexity or simplicity, crowdedness or emptiness, scale, situation, expectation, drama, familiarity, repetition/reflection, are all emotionally and psychically operative. Moreover these exist necessarily in conjunction with the time-qualities of memory, which the last five terms are functions of, as is any aspect of situation which may be known while it may or may not be immediately visible, or even may be made to be forgotten.

All this without beginning to include the culturally referential, and/or, given its possibility, lack of it.

In proscenium theatre these values may be represented. In site-specific theatre the actual contour of their resonance is experienced. In theatre that uses more than one site (beyond different points on one site), the movement of the mind, in the body, through the order of their successive resonances, and the resonance of the four-dimensional topography thus traced, reflects the city itself.

Like an analogue of the mind in the world and vice versa, the city is an experience of simultaneous interiority and exteriority. Mainly, YOU is walked; the city is entered out of and exited into. But *YOU – The City* is neither tour nor group. Its communicative form, like that of the still walkable city, is specifically, to use Marc Guillaume's terms, not the irradiative but the epidemic, not the broadcast but the word of mouth. Within the multiple, you are you in particular, confronting a specific discourse, and your response is responded to. Meaning is not just complex in time and space, meaning is promiscuous. Especially when released into the world, out from the hermetic viewpoint of pretense to a culture that could be single or contain an answer. *Against Agreement* was "against #1, the best, the biggest, the only, the winner, the right, the end". Being, itself, then, is promiscuous. The single is incomprehensible (meaningless?), in that comprehension requires consciousness, the beginning of dialectic. From two comes everything, including the conception of one. Meaning could only be invalidly offered by an active speaker to a passive hearer. The production of any play marries word and world, intention and interpretation bearing meaning out from the engaged contour of their meeting. The private in the public and vice versa, not as I and it, but as "you". That is why this book offers both the intended and the unintendable, whom was meant and who knows what.

***

YOU – The City

APPENDIX I

NOTES TO THE DIRECTIONS (On Performance)

Practical guidelines to actors

*Words **not** as symptoms of a psychology: method actors read the words, deduce the person, extend the person, i.e. make up **other things** the person might say. And often therefore get the words wrong. These words are **not** equivalent to a meaning; poetry is not a 'nicer' way.*

Greg asks, where does this guy live? I answered, I don't care, where do you live? Not quite the right answer. Where does you live? This guy lives somewhere between the speaker and the hearer. The psychology that informs this writing, if any, is that of the hearer, or rather that is, the psychology that informs the directing of the writing; so that even a primary level of interpretation (primary in the stage of mediation not level of familiarity with the text), the actor/speaker's, opens significance as fully as possible rather than specifying closure or pre-interpreting for the secondary interpreter, the hearer. The play between contextualization and the page, acting and the oracular, city and poem, is the place where "this guy lives".

It is also the place of seduction, not spectacle. "How the picture trembles if you draw it". Because the meaning of the piece is interdependent with the client, the actor needs no little "get-it"? actor-quirks that substitute for having given them it; what they need to convince the audience of is that they (the actors) mean it. "The effort of meaning, and meaning it".

from rehearsal notes, New York City 1988

The audience of *You – The City* is the client, part of the deal, "you". The performer, too, must become "you", not "him, her, it", till through the dramatic progress of the play the client can take on the performer's active address. For both performer and client, the play is not about yourself, nor the other, but their meeting, a meeting that is also placed in coincidence with the meeting of reality and artifice. Neither the psychology of the client nor of a character is the point, neither provocation of the former nor illustration of the latter, but the balance created between each two people.

The Grand Central Station auditions showed not only who could retain focused individual attention in a large crowd, but who could take me where I didn't know I was going, without my feeling forced or lost. During rehearsals forms of guidance are explored, each performer finding a personal manner; the least desirable are the most obvious, such as pointing, grabbing, or the "after you" gesture, because they would risk becoming intrusively repeated conceits of the piece.

Clients are involved in a given process, a planned route of which they may know nothing, and a text that is scripted though permeable; the audience is addressed, projected onto, scrutinized. They are not previously instructed either to respond or to remain silent. The game is to be discovered. These are the parameters into which the audience enter, though conditioned by how they heard; Newsday readers felt perfectly comfortable in parts of the city where they would never normally go, and Voice readers called to apologize to me that they didn't think they could go because they'd be anxious about being anxious. It's human to react differently in different situations, to different people. Clients may be silent, talkative, responsive, creative, challenging; apprehensive of what might happen to them, apprehensive of what they might betray of themselves, aggressive as a defense, cheeky, acting a role; they may feel pampered or invaded in reaction to the performers, comfortable or uncomfortable in reaction to the locations. In particular, since they are not given a set of "rules" or do not know conventions of the piece from the start, they will be initially unsure of how to behave, a vulnerable position. Those who respond often find themselves feeling less manipulated, even those who do not think their responses alter the script, even when their responses do. They will usually test the responsiveness of performers to their responses. Thus discovery occurs not so much through instruction by the other players as through creation by informed decision on the part of the clients. Neither decision is more correct (that is, to respond or not); requirement would create another passivity, in easy defense to the invasion privacy suggests. So beyond, or rather in the manner of, presenting his or her specific scene, the performer also has practical information to convey to the client.

Each performer has a dramatically important way of dealing with or encouraging response, dependent on his or her position in the progress of the piece. The performer has to communicate his or her own power in relation to the situation, since without sets, seats, and conventional theatrical distance the performer alone embodies the sign that there is a performance; he or she must also establish a relation of trust with the client in the sense that the client should feel in capable hands. At the same time the client needs to relax into the attitude that the play embraces him or her as more than a spectator, that he or she can affect the performance.

Much is suggested to the client rather than stated, though some things are clear. Many lines work doubly, written to be as true of my construing of the actual client/performer (or client/play) transaction, the transaction of any second-person address, as of a possible fictional construction. The client who relaxes into the moment of the play, allowing the text and the structure to build information that need not be retained consciously, will probably derive more from the experience than one who tries to figure out "what it is about".

The text is primarily a specific artifice, though written with the awareness that it derives its life from performance and reactions to it. Some written lines were assumed to be "breaking character". Chance words on the street were often thought to have been written. Many lines are written in reply to invisible anticipated responses, so when clients voice their replies, the next line may seem more improvised than it in fact is, and if clients do not reply aloud, they often feel that their minds are being read; the dialogue is between the lines of the monologue.

The text itself contains methods or points of becoming client-specific: variables and droppables are marked in each script, and particular interruption/improvisation strategies are given (page viii).

For both interruption/improvisation strategies and for the general tenor of a scene, its attitude to the client, there are two factors to consider: the apparent personality of the client and his or her emotional reactions, and the point that the scene occupies in the development of the play. Some clients can take a greater sense of danger or of realism than others, while some need to be reassured, either within the apparent fiction or by its fictionality.

The drama of the play is the development of a sense of involvement on the part of the client, leading to the opportunity to exercise it. Although each performer can seldom overhear what the client is experiencing at the hands of other performers, it is crucially important that the performer be aware of their own role in the unfolding of the client's experience. The following comments are guidelines to that practical development, rather than directions to the scenes, or than critical commentary.

***

The roles of the scenes in the structure of the client's experience

Structurally, the first act consists of single archetypes, whose recognizability and variation set a number of options in terms of response. In fact the order of performers C through F may be varied.

The first performer is unscripted, a bridge between reality and the play; the idea of response is suggested by the questionnaire given by this performer, the receptionist, which contains a question from each scene, so that if the question is recognized later, a reply has already been considered. The text of the first scripted performer (the executive) is cryptic and therefore distancing, to establish the fact of artifice, specifically in the text; immediately following the prologue-receptionist, who is completely responsive within that role as normally found, the scene throws the client in the deep end, as it were, to make it clear that this is now no longer a chat, not psychodrama, but a play into which there is no requirement to enter other than to be present. The apparent persona does not speak in character but behaves so, from a position of power. There are questions in this text, but largely rhetorical.

The second scene, the consumed consumer, is also distancing, not because of poetic density, but because the client necessarily adopts an ironic stance towards the obvious artifice of the juxtapositions and their TV-advertising origins; yet the artifice and humor can allow him or her to reply within the convention of each isolated context.

In the third scene, the mirror of forgetfulness, possible connotations of voyeurism are reversed, remaining just this side of the object, so that the client is caught, and exists, in the act of looking; but at what—the performer confronts the client with his or her own image while at the same time encouraging clients to lose themselves.

The fourth, the derelict or street person (note that both US and English terms identify, though differently, the human being with the physical urban context), is an invasive, accusatory, over-familiar role but distanced by a more psychological style of writing and acting, to the point of a strange mix of identification and embarrassment.

The fifth, the excommunicado confessor, represents another attitude to power and another form of it, so that the relation to the performer is again complex. Like many of the performers, he or she seems to establish sides to an argument without it being clear on which side either performer or client belong; "you" is not only the client being addressed, but also "one" in general, and by extension, oneself; accusation entails identification. For the confessor, the "you" is also larger, even transcendent, though the nameless power thus addressed (and thus created) might easily be the same visceral urban monster that the derelict yells at and yet participates in.

So the first act has an expository function both formally (to create the expectation of the basic form of meeting which the rest of the piece can then play with and complicate) and in presenting possible relationships and behaviors to the client (which he or she can then play with). As in the rest of the piece, ambulatory encounters are alternated with static ones, for reasons of the physical pacing of the client.

The cab ride not only separates the play's two geographical sets of locations, but also separates the introductory linear series of scenes from the loop of the rest of the piece. For the client, it provides a relieving distance at this point, since there is less text (the driver also has to drive), allowing a more relaxed response, since the eye contact has been deflected into address in the rear-view mirror, and since the text itself is fairly conversational, with that disinterested inquisitiveness and informativeness associated with the always limited encounter of the taxi. Its structural function as Parodos (see script), the entry of the chorus in Greek drama (though here displaced), is a clue to its role as commentary.

The Interacts, in some ways, have a similar role; but the word refers as much to the English verb "to interact" as to the French "entr'acte", theatrical interval, placing relation during separation. The first interact and Act II are symmetrical to the third interact and Act IV, structurally and in various references. Though references to the fourth act will not be apparent during the performance of the second, the performers of each (H, the agent and J, the minder) should be aware of the correspondences. In fact there are various cross-references, even repeated lines, throughout the piece, with which the speakers should be familiar in order to make reverberate. Both H and J prepare the client for the crossover, the first obvious aberration in the basic form of encounter, though H's client will be less aware. Both are longer than all previous encounters, and conspiratorial, H's being particularly sympathetic, emotionally on the client's side, though fictionally/structurally not so. Moreover, from this point on in the piece, the words "I" and "me" are more featured to balance the relationships and entail the client's complicity. The client begins to play a similar role to the performer. The openness to response initiated by the cab ride continues, though within a text with more fictionally suggestive direction. The second act, including the crossover, plays the role of complication.

The second interact is another deliberately cryptic scene, not so much within the sentences but in their connections, and again in order to re-establish the artifice of the play. The client has just been left alone for a moment with another client, who may or may not have played performer, and said who knows what, laying the control of the piece wide open. So while the many questions in the text of the second Interact do encourage response, the performer is clearly in control of the motivation of their subject-matter. The basic form of encounter is also reaffirmed, since it will be again blown apart in the house. To a certain extent, the interact is also designed to give little away about the role/persona of this performer before reaching the house with him or her. This performer is going to be with the client for almost three times as long as the basic encounter.

Clearly the house is structurally central, though the client will probably not yet know that the play will subsequently complete the loop to the crossover. The effect of suddenly seeing two performers play together is both complicating and distancing (see Why You? above), at times an illustration of the client's own predicament, at times instructive about it. The performing becomes acting, not just because of the distance, but because of the costumes and the switching around of specific roles; the performers are acting acting. The whole act is rapid, illusory. Artifice and theatre are foregrounded, with a darkness to counter the presence of the other client. But eye contact and involvement of the client continue; the intensity of relationship must not be lost in this act, simply complicated. Even when there is little room for reply, projection (in the psychological, not theatrical sense) should be entertaining and instructive rather than an imposition.

One of the four-person scenes (or three-actor scenes if the client is considered as still audience, with the other client as performer), the Her and It scene, has dramatic difference between characters, while the other, with Him and Him, plays duplication; both are possible strategies for the client. Since a performer while addressing the other performer speaks to or at least includes the client who entered (or was there) with the other performer, the quadrant of identification is complete; based on positions of speaking across the others rather than dividing into two conversations, the relative positions are continually varied to keep this dynamic. But the impossibility of hearing all the text, since some of it is operatically simultaneous, forces the client occasionally to concentrate on maintaining a specific relationship.

In the scenes with two clients and one performer, played at a speed with little room for reply, each client sees the performer enact responses, as if to the other client, as if they came from the client. When the other client is taken away, the subsequent monologue plays upon the fact of long acquaintance; the scene is in some sense intimate, yet cynical and knowing. The actor is describing the client's attempts at artifice and resistance while enacting them in the costume change. Fictionally, this works as a seduction distanced perhaps by role-playing; but it is also a description of the reciprocal relationship between a performer and his or her audience, encouraging equivalence in action by pointing out passivity in desire. Its crisis is allowable by being cut short by the entry of the next client-performer pair; the scene is not yet set for the client's performance. While the remainder of the house cycle is now clearer to the client, the telephone call is a further mystery that prepares the client to return to the outside world.

150

J's immediate role with the third interact and fourth act is to effect this return. The fictional relationship to the client, that of the performer's being the client's minder, is gradually undermined to the point almost of reversal, as power is invested in the client in more than a fictional sense. The italicized lines in J's text are those that build this explicit movement. Where H's text was interjected with a burst of honest sympathy, drawing the client towards the performer, J's has a outburst of challenge, pushing the client. Then each performer emotionally extricates her or himself. Then J reaches the textual climax of the play. The word "you" is what is handed to the client, and disappears from the text, which becomes more abstract as well as less personal. It is not the client's self that is revealed but his or her power of communication, of performance. The real climax of the play is then the unwritten moment when this power is exercised (even in refraining) in the meeting with the other client.

The final scripted performers use, but do not insist on, the word "you". There are two performers, with a musicality of text, opening out the intensity. In the section of their text that is the fourth interact, their commentary is "We don't know what you did." Again they are clearly artificial to follow the moment of the absence of script, but are explicit in their instructions for the telephone call. The call is a structural reinforcement, echoing with distance and instruction the client's role in completing the loop.

The final performer's role as epilogue is symmetrical to the other un-scripted scene of the prologue, easing the client back out of the play. He or she too really needs to know what the client has been through.

The Exodos or exit of the chorus is last of all, the commentary (now the clients are the chorus) between all who meet at the end being considered part of the piece, relationship carried on, points of view deepened and exchanged. Performers may join the clients.

***

summer 1989

YOU – The City

APPENDIX II

NOTES TO THE DIRECTIONS (On Structure)

1a. Client Flow: – structure

Client flow is one of the two types of movement within You, the other being the "choreography" of the routes of the performers. The Itinerary (page xiii) describes the order of encounters from the client's point of view.

The Story (page ix) mentions the basic form of these encounters, which is as follows: each client meets in a certain place a performer who takes him or her to another place where he or she is passed on to another performer, and so on. Here the evolution of that base form in the course of the play will be developed.

During the encounter the performer addresses the client with a text specific to that scene. Improvisation on that text will have been extensively rehearsed so that client response can be incorporated in ways particular to each performer's relationship with the client. However, there is no insistence or even necessary expectation that the client participate verbally in the encounter, and the texts are basically conceived as monologues pretending to be dialogues.

Having passed on a client, the performer returns to meet a new client at the place where the encounter began, and the scene is repeated. (Of course, if the scene is static or contained this place may be the same place at which the previous client was passed on.) Thus there is a constant flow of clients through the piece, and scenes in different parts of the play are simultaneous. This allows YOU to be economically manageable, as well as allowing further complications.

This fact is not part of the client's experience until the scene at the Courts, where a performer apparently exchanges clients with another performer; in fact the client in the earlier scene is joining a client from a later scene while the two performers come together. This will dawn on the more advanced client, who may or may not reveal or exploit his or her new status. Then they are joined by two more performers, one of whom has been watching just in case, and they go their separate ways as two performer--client couples once again.

Between these two scenes that meet, the client is taken to a house where

152

another performer-client couple is met and a dialogue pretending to be two dialogues takes place. The more advanced client receives a telephone call. Then the more advanced performer leaves and the two clients and remaining performer have a three-actor scene. Yet another performer arrives and takes the other client away. Client and performer are alone for a short speech, and another less advanced performer-client couple arrive. A second four-person scene takes place, echoing dramatically but emotionally different to the scene that took place when our client first arrived at the house. Our now more advanced client receives a telephone call from a performer met earlier (or a more advanced client who, having reached Act V, has almost finished the piece and has been offered the choice of attempting by persuasion to alter the course of the action), after which he or she finds that the performer with whom he or she arrived at the house has now left. There is a three actor scene which is not the same as but complementary to the previous one (its poetically literal opposite). The performer who seemed to be a client crossing our client in the exchange scene arrives and takes him or her back to the courts at the end from which they were previously left.

The more advanced client waits for the less advanced one at this second side of the courts, and the two are left alone for a moment, how long depending on whether anything interesting seems to be happening between them. The following interact returns to the base encounter form, with the less advanced client being taken first. It is at this point that our (more advanced) client is offered an explicit choice, upon which depends whether or not he or she has an Act V, that is, make the telephone call to whoever is the more advanced client at the apartment. If the choice is positive, our client can affect the course of the action of the play for subsequent clients.

In the final location, once the client has been admitted to the cafe, he or she may remain there and meet other clients, direction and production staff, and the remote monitors of the performance, who are in telephone contact with the monitor performers in scenes at regular intervals throughout the journey, ready to dispatch fake clients to the apartment and crossover scenes to camouflage gaps in real client flow.

The above complexities depend upon the establishment of the base form in Act I in midtown so that they are understood as variations or that the base form is buried and expected.

1b. Client Flow: – diagram

PROLOGUE

ACT I
Scene i   Reception!
           !...A....!

           ! Office!
           !...B...!

Scene ii   > TimesSq
           !...C....!

Scene iii !Harlequin!
           !....D....!

Scene iv   > 46 St!
           !...E...!

Scene v   !St Luke's!
           !....F....!

PARODOS   > Car !
           !..G..!

FIRST   > Courts > X
INTERACT/ !.H....!..X/   X with c1
ACT II

SECOND   /! > !10th Ave !
INTERACT   !...I1.....!

ACT III ~ !I1 !
           !c4 I1 I1 ! I13 c6!
           !I2.!c4!...!I1I1.! c6 I3!

THIRD   > Courts > X
INTERACT/ !.J....!...!..X/   X
ACT IV

FOURTH   /X > !X > !
INTERACT/ X...K.../ X T
(ACT V)   with c9

EXODOS/   > cafe
EPILOGUE   !....L......M+

(where the path followed is that of client c 5, that is,
with the first client being c 1, and so on.)

X   T = (time of) telephone call
X = crossover
X

... = one minute   > = moving scene

2. Performer Shuttles: structure and base diagrams

Performer shuttles are the second of the two types of movement within YOU, the first being client flow. The movement is referred to as shuttles because, as described in the last section, having passed on a client at the end of an encounter, each performer returns to meet a new client at the place where the encounter began.

The base form of each performer shuttle, including the trajectory with the client to the handoff point and the return alone to the pickup point, is completed within a ten-minute unit of time. The assumption is normally made that a performer accompanying a client will take longer to cover any trajectory as he or she would take alone. Thus the base form can be described as in the diagram that follows:

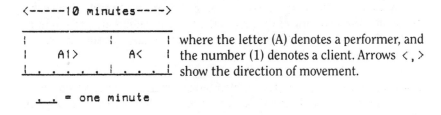

```
<-----10 minutes---->
```

A1>	A<	where the letter (A) denotes a performer, and the number (1) denotes a client. Arrows < , > show the direction of movement.

```
. . . = one minute
```

This form relates to other clients in the following way:

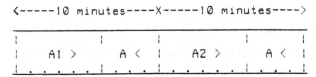

```
<-----10 minutes----X-----10 minutes---->
```

where the number (2) denotes a second client,

and to other performers in this way:

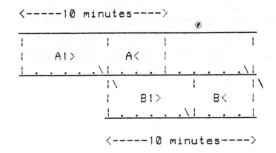

```
<-----10 minutes---->
```

where the letter (B) denotes a second performer. The slash (\) left to right shows the point of client changeover.

```
<-----10 minutes---->
```

Note that while a scene may take, say, six or seven or ten minutes, clients always arrive at an encounter at intervals of ten minutes. Synchronization is therefore a function of the moment of passing on the client.

Thus the clock time of A's pickup and B's handoff are not relevant to each other, as long as they coincide every ten minutes for A's handoff to B's pickup. Thus while A's scene involves a six minute trajectory and a four-minute return, B's might easily involve a seven minute trajectory as long as B's return was then reduced to three minutes, and as long as the length of that trajectory was decided in conjunction with Performer C to specify the subsequent changeover time to suit C's intervals.

Ten minutes, then, is the base unit of time from which the timing of the entire piece is calculated. If timing within that unit is found to be inappropriate for the particular distance of any scene, as, for example, if the above six minute trajectory of B's has to be given seven minutes, it can be readjusted to the timing of the rest of the piece by sliding that ten minute unit to fit the new changeover point. And prior or subsequent scenes can follow that adjustment.

However, this becomes more complicated when the changeover points of more than two scenes have to coincide, as for for Performers H through K at the crossover, which prevents those scenes it contains (I and J) from having an open end (see below for details).

* * *

All of the scenes follow or are some type of variation on this base form, as follows:

The Prologue, and Exodos with Epilogue are, from the performer's point of view, static and open-ended. In other words, the performer remains in the same place to allow for a buildup of arriving and departing performers respectively. In the Prologue, this means that clients can be held until the appropriate moment for the timing to begin Act I, scene i. In the Exodos with Epilogue, it means that they can remain for as long as they like, while other clients complete the piece.

Scenes iii and v of Act I, though they conform to the timing of the piece, are given a full ten-minute unit since the performer is with the client from beginning to end of that time in a contained area, with the changeover at each end happening in the same place.

Moving scenes such as *Scenes i, ii and iv of Act I*, and the car scene in the *Parodos* that follows it, as well as and the *Fourth Interact with or without Act V*, may be doubled (or even tripled) in *total* shuttle timing (that is, including the return), depending on the distance to be covered. So an ambulatory scene could take, say, twelve minutes for the encounter and eight minutes for the return; and the car scene could take, say, twenty minutes for the ride and ten minutes to return. In order for client flow to continue uninterrupted with these delays, performers for these scenes would be duplicated (or triplicated), thus:

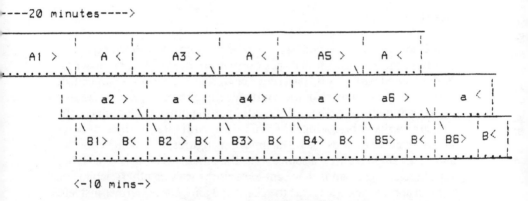

and so on, where A and a are different performers covering the same twelve-minute scene with alternating clients, and B has a regular six-minute scene with every client.

Acts II, III and IV and their preceding interacts involve complex variations on the base form. The resultant scenes from the clients' point of view are described narratively in the actual script and directions for the play. Here the scenes will be described first as base forms or roles, and then their distribution between performers will be explained.

***

157

First Interact

The first base form of these sections is simple, being a five-minute walk from the car drop-off point, into the playground, and over to the basketball courts until the point where two others are seen approaching. This can be drawn thus:

```
<-----10 minutes---->
_____
¦           ¦           ¦
¦  Hn p>[ ,    H [<p    ¦
¦ . . . . ¦ . . . . ¦
```

H = performer H
n = client n
p = southern entrance to playground
[= southern entrance to courts

Act II

This is followed by a second base form by the same performer, separated only from the first because of its position within the structure of the script. In the second part of this trajectory, Act II, scene i, performer and client hesitate at the beginning of the courts for three minutes, as they see two figures symmetrical to their own position at the other side of the courts, who are similarly hesitating. The walk then continues for three minutes (Act II, scene ii) towards the two approaching figures; then both performer and client stop at a little distance from the others, as do they. This totals six minutes. The client is then sent towards the waiting others, while one of them approaches, walks past the client and joins the performer just left. This crossover is only momentary, and for the performer can be considered part of the return. This four-minute return is therefore in the presence of another person, while the client continues on a symmetrical walk with the person he or she has just joined.

(In fact, unknown to the client, the person who has just joined the performer is another performer, and the person whom the client has just joined is a client participating in a later scene of the play. This will be clarified later on.)

For the moment, this can be drawn thus:

```
<-----10 minutes---->
_____
¦       ¦     ¦  HJ   ¦
¦Hn [   Hn[>X¦  >  H>[  ¦
¦ . ¦ . . ¦ . . ¦ . . ¦
              x
```

J = performer J, who has joined performer H
[= southern end of courts
X = beginning of distance for crossover
x = crossover

158

Note that in the script the crossover and the time spent with the client at the other (northern) side of the Courts, though not considered to take any time from the point of view of performer arrival and departure (this is because all the performers involved in the crossover need to be there while the clients are alone), are considered as a separate scene (Act II, scene iii), so that for the client this last base form covers all of Act II.

So, since the same performer (H) appears in both the first Interact and in Act II, that performer's two sets of scenes, totaling eleven minutes of trajectory and nine minutes of return, can be drawn together, with of course the duplicate performer necessitated by the length of the double role, thus (with different clients shown as n and n + 1):

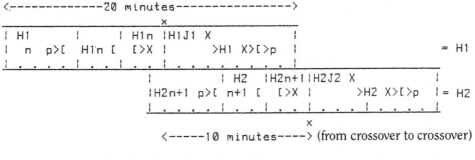

```
<------------20 minutes--------------->
                      x
_____
! H1        !       ! H1n !H1J1  X            !
!  n   p>[  H1'n [   [>X !        >H1  X>[>p   !                = H1
! . . . . ! . . ! . . . . ! . . . . . . . !
                      !         ! H2  !H2n+1!H2J2  X            !
                      !H2n+1 p>[ n+1 [   [>X !        >H2  X>[>p   != H2
                      ! . . . . ! . . ! . . ! . . . . . ! . . . . !
                                        x
                      <-----10 minutes----> (from crossover to crossover)

<-----11 minutes-------> (H's trajectory from car/entrance to crossover)
```

J's complete scene will be explained with Act IV.

Second Interact and Act III

There are basically three performers involved in the scenes at the apart-ment, including the Interact preceding it which takes the client from the northern end of the courts to the house. In terms of time, these performers also cover three base forms between each. However, since two of these trajectories are contained, i.e. at the apartment, only one return is con-tained within the thirty minutes of their total base form. The trajectory of this first base form constitutes for the client the Second Interact:

Second Interact:

This brings the client from the other (northern) side of the crossover at the courts to the apartment, taking ten minutes, and so implying a duplicate base form with a ten-minute return to the end of the tracks:

159

<----10 minutes----->

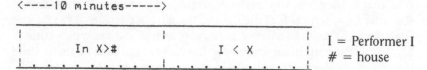

```
<----10 minutes----->
┌─────────────────────────────────────────────┐
│         In X>#              I < X            │   I = Performer I
└ . . . . . . . . . . . . . . . . . . . . . . ┘   # = house
```

At the end of the return (or at the beginning of the trajectory) Performer I oversees unseen the two clients alone at the crossover before picking up the less advanced client for the next trajectory.

Act III:

The above twenty minutes leaves ten out of Performer I's thirty minute triplicate unit for the action at the apartment. However, in fact the return without the client should not require the full ten minutes allowed for it above, so four of those minutes are absorbed into the time at the apartment, giving performers more time there with clients. One total cycle of trajectory and return for one Performer I can therefore be drawn:

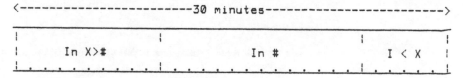

```
<--------------------------30 minutes-------------------------->
┌────────────────────────────────────────────────────────────────┐
│      In X>#                  In #                 I < X         │
└ . . . . . . . . . . . . . . . . . . . . . . . . . . . . . . . . ┘
```

Each of the three Performer I's in this Interact and Act performs this cycle, which gives a triplicate form like this:

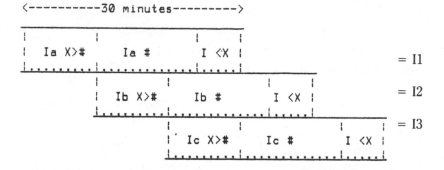

```
<----------30 minutes---------->
┌──────────────────────────────────┐
│   Ia X>#     Ia #      I <X │
└ . . . . . . . . . . . . . . . ┘              = I1
    │   Ib X>#     Ib #      I <X │
    └ . . . . . . . . . . . . . . ┘            = I2
        │   Ic X>#     Ic #      I <X │
        └ . . . . . . . . . . . . . . ┘        = I3
```

The extra four minutes at the apartment therefore overlap time at the beginning and end of the visit with each of the other Performer I's respectively, as well as with those performers' clients. Thus scenes can be created that include two performers and two clients, and one performer and two clients, as well as other variations.

Since Act III constitutes a distinct form from the rest of the encounters, the structural and choreographic details of the scenes at the apartment will be explained separately following the structural description of the rest of the piece.

***

Third Interact and Act IV

These form an almost symmetrical structure to the first Interact and Act II. The third Interact brings the client from the apartment back to the northern end of the courts, and on into Act IV:

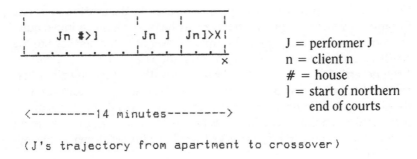

J = performer J
n = client n
# = house
] = start of northern end of courts

(J's trajectory from apartment to crossover)

Scene i of Act IV reflects that of Act II, with performer (the same one as in the preceding interact) and client walking towards the two who are approaching, and then stopping at a slight distance at the same time as the others do. In scene ii, however, it is the performer and not the client who walks over towards the others, and the client who remains waiting for the person approaching.

In scene iii the performer passes from Act IV to join the performer in Act II, while from the clients' point of view the acts also coincide briefly (both scene iii's) as an encounter between two clients. The activity of the clients does not fall under the description of the performer shuttles, but in terms of performance control, one of them (the client in Act IV) will probably have figured out his or her role with respect to the other client as an apparent performer, and the consequent freedom, power or responsibility, since the client in Act II is unlikely to realize unless the other one makes it clear; but the fact that the more advanced client knows that they will shortly be reabsorbed back into their separate itineraries, and also the fact, of which he or she may be unaware, that one of the performers from Act III is watching, makes it possible to describe the scene basically as a return to the northern end of the courts. For the two performers, the scene is exactly the same scene as in Act II. Thus for the performer of Act IV the whole Act, with the third Interact preceding it, will look like this:

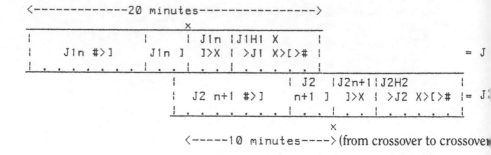

```
       <-------------20 minutes--------------->
                           x
    _____
    !                    !    ! Jin  !J1H! X         !
    !     Jln #>]        Jln ]  ]>X ! >J1 X>[>#  !              = J
    !._._._._._._._._.!_._!_._!_._!_._._._._._!
                       !         ! J2  !J2n+1!J2H2        !
                       ! J2 n+1 #>]  n+1 ]  ]>X ! >J2 X>[>#  != J
                       !._._._._._._._.!_._!_._!_._._._._._!
                                             x
                       <-----10 minutes----> (from crossover to crossover
```

Note that the return brings this performer back to the apartment in one five-minute return, in spite of the fact that he or she has continued quite far from there as starting point, by crossing over from the northern to the southern end of the courts. This is based on the assumption that Performer J can nevertheless exit from the playground without retracing all of Performer H's steps (and, in order to give the semblance of going back through the piece, without retracing his or her own steps), and that the apartment is situated at a point where distances are fairly equal from the apartment to both the playground exits. This exit would be for performer J only, not for clients.

It can be traced in the total form of the Performer Shuttle diagram that the structures of Acts II, III and IV fit together so that if a performer J has passed a client at the crossover during that client's Act II, scene ii, while the client is presumably unaware that he or she is approaching another client, then it will be the same performer J that brings that client from the apartment to the tracks for Act IV. (This is since J Performers alternate, and the less advanced client at the crossover is four clients behind the more advanced one). Thus the client is made to think about what really happened at the tracks before actually arriving there once more; this, coupled with the experience at the apartment as well as the text, should prepare the client for his or her moment of secret glory.

The crossover structure of Acts II and IV can be drawn more graphically so as to include the client and performer with whom the exchange is being made, showing their physical relationships, and showing how Acts II and IV are structurally identical counterparts. (See pages 55 and 117.)

162

Fourth Interact and Act V

Act V may be contained within the Fourth Interact, these two together constituting a scene of normal base length. But since Act V, the telephone call from this client to the client in the fourth scene at the apartment (Act III), is optional, the performer may simply pass the client directly on to the exodos and epilogue, which are really simultaneous, static, and open-ended at both beginning and end. However, time for the telephone call is limited to about a minute for reasons pertinent to the each of two scenes it links: in Act III the client on the phone will be have to re-enter the following scene; and in the Fourth Interact Performers K may be waiting, since because of the moment it is timed to coincide with in Act III, the telephone call has to happen along the trajectory of Performers K rather than at the changeover to Performer L, so that that minute is included in the time for the Fourth Interact. If the client chooses not to make the call, this time is used by one of the two Performers K as a monitor performer; the performer should contact performer A by telephone, in order to let him or her know that since the client is not making the telephone call to Act III, performer A should do so, using the text otherwise given in the program (which clients receive on finishing), "The beginning in the middle that may have to wait till the end."

***

Act III – House Play, with 3 I's and Them

Act III, therefore, has a cyclical structure, into which clients enter at alternating symmetrical points. They also leave at alternating symmetrical points, but entries and exits do not coincide, so they overlap at the apartment. Each client, however, witnesses all five scenes, and encounters all three I Performers. The directions given in the script are therefore for a

Performer Shuttles:
diagram of total form showing shuttles for clients 5-8

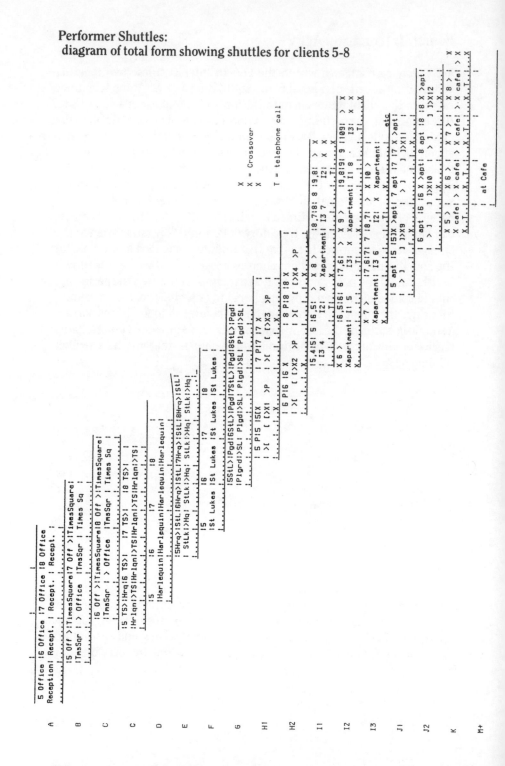

3. Act III – Apartment exits and entrances

Out of the complete cycles of the three Performer I's, the details of Act III, that is the scenes at the apartment, can be focused on. This can be done showing the scenes experienced from the point of view of three clients rather than performers, since a client remains at the apartment for one scene after the departure of the performer with whom he or she arrived there. A performer has four scenes (fourteen minutes) at the apartment, therefore, while a client has five (seventeen minutes). However, the cycle within the house repeats itself every ten minutes as each new set of performer and client arrives.

That ten minutes is divided into three scenes, marked by the arrival or departure of a client or a performer. Client and performer arrive together, finding a client and a performer already there.

After four minutes the performer who was already at the house leaves the room. Three minutes later the client who was already at the house is taken out either by that performer leaving the house, to be handed to Performer J outside, or by Performer J himself, leaving the client inside alone for another three minutes with the performer with whom he or she arrived there. At that point another performer and client arrive and the cycle begins again, our client's and performer's scene iv being the new pair's scene i, so that our client and performer are now in the position of the client and performer who were there when ours arrived, but with a reversal in the point of view of the text (the Gender Alteration chart below also embeds, from the client's point of view, a certain subject/object switch). When our Performer leaves at the end of this four-minute scene, our client is left with the new pair for his or her scene v, their scene ii, which complements his or her scene ii, with a semantic rather than a syntactic reversal.
So, if Performer I1 and Client a arrive at the apartment to find Performer I2 and Client b already there:

```
                                                       scene
! i  ! ii! iii !  iv  ! v !                            performer
! I1,I2   I1      I1    I3,I1   I3 !                    client
!a. . .b!a.b! .a. . !c. . .a!c.a!
                     !  i  ! ii! iii !  iv  ! v !       scene
                     ! I3,I1   I3      I3    I2,I3   I2 !performer
                     !c. . .a!c.a! .c. . !d. . .c!d.c!  client
                                       !  i  ! ii! iii !  iv  ! v !
  scene                                ! I2,I3   I2      I2    I2,I1   I1 !
  performer                            !d. . .c!d.c! .d. . !d. . .e!d.e!
  client
```

***

165

client experiencing the scenes in the order: i,ii,iii,iv,v; the subsequent client will experience them in the order iv,v,iii,i,ii. Scene iii is given once, being constant since client and performer are once again alone.

The cycle is different for performers (triple rather than double because of the trip to the playground for the Second Interact) to the cycle for clients, text and costumes. So the Performer numbers 1,2,3 are also an example, and could be equally 2,3,1 or 3,1,2.

There are four sets of clothes: Her, It, Him and Him. Him and Him are identical.

Gender Alternation; (who I acts)

As mentioned above, while the structure of exits and entrances at the apartment works on a ten minute cycle, the text works on a twenty minute cycle, the four-person scene between Her and It alternating with the one between Him and Him, with their corresponding subsequent three-person scenes. Each client's visit there is sixteen minutes long, since the remaining four minutes of the cycle are simply the repeated scene iii. However, since there are three Performer I's, each on a thirty-minute cycle because of the trip to and from the playground (see Second Interact), each time a Performer I returns to the apartment, it will be to a different four-person scene. There will be no confusion as to which, as the Performer will be dressed either as Her or as Him. Similarly, in scene iii, there is no confusion as to the new clothing, as there will only be one set there hanging unoccupied.

So it will be a full hour before any one Performer I repeats the same part in a four-person monologue, and in this way therefore the Performer I's are in fact on a six-fold cycle, learning both sides of both dialogues. The reversal is important to remember during any improvisation at the apartment.

The reversal also refers for Performer I to which monologue for the three-person scene he or she takes on any one visit. Thus one of the monologues occurs in scene ii for the one client while it is simultaneously scene iv for the other, so a different monologue must be given for the former client's scene iv. In the client script these scenes are given a fixed order: crossover, interact, i,ii,iii,iv,v; but in the scripts of the Performer I's they would have to be given: crossover, interact, ia,ii,iii,iva, return, crossover, interact, ivb,v,iii,ib, return. Of course, ia and ivb are identical, except that the Performer takes the other part in the dialogue; similarly with iva and ib. There is no change from one cycle to another in the interact and scene iii (other than the costume itself) since they are heard only once by each client.

Gender Alternation Chart

Scene	Performers	Clients	Performer J(ust Visiting to Take Client To Tracks)
i	I1(It),I2(Her) swap, I1 leaves as Her	a,b	
ii	I2(It)	a,b	
			J1
iii	I2(It, becomes Him)	b	
iv	I2(Him),I3(Him) I2 leaves as Him	b,c	
v	I3(Him)	b,c	
			J2
iii	I3(Him, becomes It)	c	
i	I3(It),I1(Her) swap, I3 leaves as Her	c,d	
ii	I1(It)	c,d	
			J1
iii	I1(It, becomes Him)	d	
iv	I1(Him),I2(Him) I1 leaves as Him	d,e	
v	I2(Him)	d,e	
			J2
iii	I2(Him, becomes It)	e	
i	I2(It),I3(Her) swap, I2 leaves as Her	e,f	
ii	I3(It)	e,f	
			J1
iii	I3(It, becomes Him)	f	
iv	I3(Him),I1(Him) I3 leaves as Him	f,g	
v	I1(Him)	f,g	
			J2
iii	I1(Him, becomes It)	g	
i	I1(It),I2(Her)	g,h	

***

4. Other Performer and Client Roles: Monitor Performers, Blanks, Fake Clients, and Standby Appointments

Monitor Performers

Certain performers, either those at crucial points or those whose timing allows, have the further role of Monitor Performers (see Epilogue). These are principally Performer A, the YOU receptionist, at more or less any moment; whichever of the Performer B's, the YOU executives, are not actually with a client; if necessary Performer D, even while with a client, as she is indoors near a telephone; Performer H, during the return, as liaison between the car and the first area (for production purposes, though not in the structure of the script, referred to as the first half) of the piece, and the entire second half via the crossover; Performer I at the apartment, between the end of the fourth scene and leaving, and obviously never when a telephone call is due for a client; Performers K, as they link with Performer L and the end of the piece, and can even split up if necessary. All performers should be able to relay information to prior and subsequent performers, so that it can be passed to principal Monitor Performers, either on returns or furtively at a changeover.

Fake Clients

At the beginning and end of the day, there is of course no more advanced client than the first one and no less advanced client than the last, to meet them at the crossover and in the apartment. Fake clients are used at these times. These would usually be Monitor Performers from the Epilogue. One fake client is needed for the first four and last four crossovers, and one for the first and last arrivals in the apartment, since of clients meeting at the crossover one is four behind the first.

Performers K will also need to make three fake though actual telephone calls to the apartment at the beginning of the day, though the first of these will speak to a fake client. Similarly, at the end of the day, the Performer I's will need to receive as fake clients two calls there from the last real clients in Act V.

Real clients who have already completed the piece and are at the cafe for the epilogue, or even who have completed it on a previous day, may make good fake clients, at least good fake less advanced clients, their main role being to act as if naive.

However, the fake more advanced clients at the beginning of the day's performances have important roles in that the real client identifies with them. The fake client at the house may be the first apparent peer that the

168

real client is aware of meeting, and thus the real may take his or her cue from the fake's behavior (whether to play, to reply, to improvise, to move, to challenge, to retreat, to identify, and so on).

And while the fake client at the crossover may or may not at the time of meeting be guessed by the real client to be a supposed client, nevertheless when the real one finds her or himself in that position, its possibilities can have been suggested by the then remembered behavior of the fake. Perhaps the (fake) more advanced client could (pretend to) pretend to be a performer in such a way that when the real client (thinks he or she) realizes on becoming the more advanced that the other was in fact (though not really) another client, that (pretense at) pretense would have been (supposedly) transparent and simple enough in retrospect for the real client to exploit a similar strategy (at the first level) of role playing.

Moreover, as *the* point of client-client contact, the crossover meeting could become a catalytic site of rumor (as could, with greater impunity, the telephone call).

Blanks

If by chance a client with an appointment fails to show up, a blank is sent through the piece. For performers in the first half, including the car, this means that they still need to make their trajectory to pass that fact on to the next performer. For performers in the second half, the word has to be spread in a less linear way because of the crossover; so the fact is passed from Performer H to Performer J, from Performer G (the car) to Performers K and possibly I and J, and from Performers K to the Performer I's and to Performer L.

From there the Monitor Performers at the end are alerted to send out a fake client, first to perform the crossover to meet the more advanced client coming back from the apartment, and then with Performer I to the apartment to walk in on the more advanced client there and stay for that client's scenes iv and v; then the fake client stays for the next real client's scenes i and ii, then returns to meet yet another client at the second side of the crossover.

If two subsequent blanks are sent through, two fake clients are needed, though one can do both sets of crossover scenes (being handed back from Performers K to Performer H) and one can do both sets of apartment scenes, as long as all the duplicate and triplicate performers involved keep to the appropriate physical places on their cycles.

Three or four subsequent blanks can also be dealt with by two fake clients, one at the crossover and another in the apartment. However, more than four blanks, or odd combinations of blanks can not be dealt with this way, as there is a risk of the real client meeting the same fake client twice, in the guise of different positions in the piece. For example, two subsequent blanks are preferable to a blank followed by a real client followed by a blank, as this necessitates two fake clients doing the full route from crossover to apartment to crossover; otherwise the client would get the same fake client, who would have gone out and come back in, for scenes i and iv of Act III. It is up to Performer A to avoid a blank-real-blank, since clients should overlap at reception, and can be held there for a delay of the ten-minute interval before being handed on to Performer B.

Standby Appointments

Ticketing should be done in advance, both in order to avoid blanks as well as because the office should not become a box-office but retain its ambiguous business identity. However, in order to cover for the unavoidable, a ticketing system similar to that of standby airline tickets can be used: prospective clients unable to make an appointment due to either full bookings or prohibitive prices may come to the office prepared to wait for eventual blanks whose place they can take, understood that they may have to wait till the end of the day, or, if there are too many standby hopefuls, it may be impossible to accommodate them that day.

***

5. Real Time and Mistakes

It is probably easiest for individual performers, while knowing their own ten, twenty or thirty minute intervals as clock times (as in the Performer/Client Timetable), to be aware of the flow of the whole piece as a rhythm (as in Performer Shuttles and Client Flow). Real-time aberrations from form are inevitable and often its test, and the following are methods of accommodating them.

Inter-performer grapevine

The crucial points of the piece are linked by telephone, but a substructure of communication from one end of the performance to the other is both practically and psychologically necessary (see guidelines for actors). Performers in the first half depend mainly on the moving scenes (Prologue, ii,iv, Parodos) for information (for example, blanks, accidents, need for performer relief or substitution, broken telephones or cars, environmental factors, local upheaval, awry timing, clients with needs), while in the second half, the loop and duplicates allow information to circulate faster. So blanks still require that performers complete their trajectory and return to starting for any new information.

Early and late pickups and handoffs

If a performer finishes his or her scene too early, it is up to the following performer to restore the timing by only taking the new client at the appropriate time; clients shouldn't overlap, to avoid being thrown into self-consciousness. In any case the former performer shouldn't leave his or her client until the latter performer has picked him or her up. If a performer is consistently too early, performers on either side can communicate this information.

Similarly, if a performer finishes his or her scene too late, it is up to the following performer to restore the timing by shortening his or her scene so that it finishes at the appropriate time. Again, if a performer is consistently too late, performers on either side can communicate this information.

Creating blanks

If for reasons beyond his or her control a performer finishes the scene later and later, which might happen to the car if the traffic is heavy, that performer can agree with other performers that a blank be created. This involves, for example, performers H missing one encounter from performer G in the car and sending a fake client to the appropriate following crossovers and apartment; performer G therefore has ten minutes (or the remainder of ten minutes, depending on how late he or she had become) to spare. So that clients do not begin to overlap with performer F while waiting at the car, the receptionist can be informed to send a blank through the first half, and all performers in the first half can accommodate their timing slightly until the flow is restored.

Mistakes are simply more unintendables, and may or may not be discussed with clients, within each performer's interruption/improvisation strategies.

␣␣*␣

6. Performer/Client Timetable: Manhattan May-June 1988

```
                                    X OVER APT        APT
A    B    C    D    E    F    G    H  H/I/J/K  I  CALL  J    K    CALL  L
                                                            4:20
                                                            4:30
                                        4:20            4:40
3:00 3:09 3:17 3:24 3:34 3:40 3:50 3:56 4:07 4:17 4:30 4:33 4:47 4:50 4:5
3:10 3:19 3:27 3:34 3:44 3:50 4:00 4:06 4:17 4:27 4:40 4:43 4:57 5:00 5:0
3:20 3:29 3:37 3:44 3:54 4:00 4:10 4:16 4:27 4:37 4:50 4:53 5:07 5:10 5:1
3:30 3:39 3:47 3:54 4:04 4:10 4:20 4:26 4:37 4:47 5:00 5:03 5:17 5:20 5:2
3:40 3:49 3:57 4:04 4:14 4:20 4:30 4:36 4:47 4:57 5:10 5:13 5:27 5:30 5:3
3:50 3:59 4:07 4:14 4:24 4:30 4:40 4:46 4:57 5:07 5:20 5:23 5:37 5:40 5:4
4:00 4:09 4:17 4:24 4:34 4:40 4:50 4:56 5:07 5:17 5:30 5:33 5:47 5:50 5:5
4:10 4:19 4:27 4:34 4:44 4:50 5:00 5:06 5:17 5:27 5:40 5:43 5:57 6:00 6:0
4:20 4:29 4:37 4:44 4:54 5:00 5:10 5:16 5:27 5:37 5:50 5:53 6:07 6:10 6:1
4:30 4:39 4:47 4:54 5:04 5:10 5:20 5:26 5:37 5:47 6:00 6:03 6:17 6:20 6:2
4:40 4:49 4:57 5:04 5:14 5:20 5:30 5:36 5:47 5:57 6:10 6:13 6:27 6:30 6:3
4:50 4:59 5:07 5:14 5:24 5:30 5:40 5:46 5:57 6:07 6:20 6:23 6:37 6:40 6:4
5:00 5:09 5:17 5:24 5:34 5:40 5:50 5:56 6:07 6:17 6:30 6:33 6:47 6:50 6:5
5:10 5:19 5:27 5:34 5:44 5:50 6:00 6:06 6:17 6:27 6:40 6:43 6:57 7:00 7:0
5:20 5:29 5:37 5:44 5:54 6:00 6:10 6:16 6:27 6:37 6:50 6:53 7:07 7:10 7:1
5:30 5:39 5:47 5:54 6:04 6:10 6:20 6:26 6:37 6:47 7:00 7:03 7:17 7:20 7:2
5:40 5:49 5:57 6:04 6:14 6:20 6:30 6:36 6:47 6:57 7:10 7:13 7:27 7:30 7:3
5:50 5:59 6:07 6:14 6:24 6:30 6:40 6:46 6:57 7:07 7:20 7:23 7:37 7:40 7:4
6:00 6:09 6:17 6:24 6:34 6:40 6:50 6:56 7:07 7:17 7:30 7:33 7:47 7:50 7:5
6:10 6:19 6:27 6:34 6:44 6:50 7:00 7:06 7:17 7:27 7:40 7:43 7:57 8:00 8:0
6:20 6:29 6:37 6:44 6:54 7:00 7:10 7:16 7:27 7:37 7:50 7:53 8:07 8:10 8:1
6:30 6:39 6:47 6:54 7:04 7:10 7:20 7:26 7:37 7:47 8:00 8:03 8:17 8:20 8:2
                                        7:47 7:57      8:10
                                        7:57           8:20
(underlined = fake)                     8:07
                                        8:17
                                    X OVER APT        APT
A    B    C    D    E    F    G    H  H/I/J/K  I  CALL  J    K    CALL  L
```

172
UNIVERSITY OF WINCHESTER LIBRARY